Miracles in Room 107

The ABC's of Childlike Faith

Sheri H. Thrower

Copyright © 2015 SHERI H. THROWER
All rights reserved. This book or any portion thereof
may not be reproduced or used in any manner whatsoever
without the express written permission of the publisher
except for the use of brief quotations in a book review.

Limits of Liability and Disclaimer of Warranty

The author and publisher shall not be liable for your misuse of this material. This book is strictly for informational and educational purposes.

The purpose of this book is to educate and entertain. The author and/or publisher do not guarantee that anyone following these techniques, suggestions, tips, ideas, or strategies will become successful. The author and/or publisher shall have neither liability nor responsibility to anyone with respect to any loss or damage caused, or alleged to be caused, directly or indirectly by the information contained in this book.

Although the author and publisher have made every effort to ensure that the information in this book was correct at press time, the author and publisher do not assume and hereby disclaim any liability to any party for any loss, damage, or disruption caused by errors or omissions, whether such errors or omissions result from negligence, accident, or any other cause. Views expressed in this publication do not necessarily reflect the views of the publisher.

Printed in the United States of America

ISBN 978-1-941749-26-5

4-P Publishing
Chattanooga, TN 37411

Sheri H. Thrower
Sheriht@aol.com
www.sheriproductions.com

Hear Sheri's music at: www.reverbnation.com/sherithrower
Free listening!

Editors: Cathy Billington/Averi Thrower
Graphic Art Design: Averi Thrower

What others are saying about Sheri:

"For over fifteen years I have asked Sheri to return as praise and worship leader for our women's retreat. She is also a guest speaker, and her workshop has been the most complimented. She has had more copies ordered than almost any other workshop leader. Sheri's communication connects."

-Ann Downing: Dove Award Winning Artist and President of "Middle Tennessee Women's Retreat" in Nashville, TN

"I've had the privilege of working first hand with Sheri in a variety of music and ministry settings. She simply does everything with excellence. She is a stellar singer, worship leader, songwriter, speaker, choir clinician, musician, and teacher. She always conducts herself with class, while keeping things fun and inspiring."

-Phil Cross: Dove Award Winning Songwriter and President of Cross Music Group in Chattanooga, TN.

Acknowledgements

Cathy Billington, my friend and editor, thank you for spending your school snow days wrapped in my words and stories, when you could've been making angel wings and sledding! Your graciousness is contagious, and beyond admirable. Your suggestions made the re-writes a joy! Your book is next.

Jeffrey Duke, thank you for the ABC chapter idea!

Friend and mentor, Stephanie Dickert, thank you for leading the way for me to write. Your book gave me the encouragement to say, "Well, I can, too!" I followed you into the land authoring where I have found myself forever addicted. Thank you for such inspiration.

Laura Brown, my S.W.A.T. class publishing coach, thank you for helping me to reach into the depths of my heart and pull out a dream that is tangible. Your motivation is anointed and powerful. I'm forever grateful for your investment into my life and dream.

Mom, dad, and sister, Andrea, thank you for understanding that I am my daddy's daughter. Preacher Dave has his book, and now Sister Sheri has hers! May the "Two Peas in a Pod Club" live on! I could not have written this book, nor lived its pages without your unconditional love and support. Thank you for understanding the hours of hibernating at my laptop, delayed returned phone calls, and a million and one calls asking, "How does this sound?" I love you from my toes!

Averi, my beautiful daughter and cover designer, no one could have done it better! Thank you for using your talent and life to honor The Lord. It means so much to have your artistic touch as everyone's first eye candy. This book is only the beginning for your graphic art designs. I love you so much.

My son, Michael, thank you for setting the example first for me. Your love of writing and consistent passion for stories has been my example. I have simply followed your lead, and I look forward to the day when I can hold an autographed copy of your bestselling books in my hands. I love you so much.

Ann Downing and our lovely friends of the "Middle Tennessee Women's Retreat", thank you for giving me a platform to share what Christ has done for me. You were the first to share in the journey to Room 107. Thank you for going there with me.

Pastor Kevin Wallace and Redemption Point Church Family, thank you for giving our family a safe place to worship and call "home."

The many friends who have prayed and cheered me on in writing my story, thank you for your "hoorah's and that-a-girl!" from the stands. Please keep the prayers coming!

My Father in Heaven, a huge lump rests in my throat as I try to find a way to say, "Thank You." Mere words aren't enough. I could make up the most beautiful words and it still wouldn't suffice. However, I know that the salty splashes of tears on the keys of my laptop are a language that You can truly understand. Although my full story is not complete, Your love for me is. And that's a story all its own. I love You, my Story and my Song.

Dedication

This book is lovingly dedicated to the wonderful children who have danced, clapped, sung songs, and daily changed the atmosphere of Room 107 and other music rooms of my career. The life song you sing of tenacity, forgiveness, love and laughter, is forever embedded in my heart. Thank *you* for teaching me. I've learned much.

To my children, Michael and Averi, I love you. Let this book be a remembrance of God's faithfulness and provision for our family through the years. Rest in knowing that it will never ever end.

Psalm 91…always.

With love,

Ms. Thrower/ a.k.a., "Ms. Froher" and Mom

About the Author

Sheri Thrower is an award winning music educator with over twenty years' experience in public education. She is a graduate of the University of Tennessee at Chattanooga, where she received her B.S. in music education. Her award-winning children's choirs have delighted audiences across the nation, and have been featured at the nation's most renowned venues that include: Radio City Music Hall/NYC, The United States Capitol/Washington, D.C., Walt Disney World/Orlando, Florida, and more.

Sheri wears many hats in the gospel music industry. As a songwriter, her original songs and arrangements have topped the gospel music charts. As a worship leader and author, she sings and speaks at Christian women's conferences across the nation. She makes her home in Georgia where she enjoys writing, choral arranging, and being a mother of two.

Preface

It's just an ordinary phone booth. He's just an ordinary man. But when he steps inside the phone booth, something miraculous takes place. With an "S" on his chest and jaw tightly set, he emerges back into society ready to conquer the world. He's anything but ordinary. He's nothing less than a superhero. He's Superman.

That's the picture of Room 107, the music room where I've taught for over ten years. And that's the picture of the wonderful children I've seen transformed when stepping through its door. They are just ordinary children, and it's just an ordinary classroom. But when they step inside the "music booth" of creativity and wonder, it transforms them into super heroes of a greater kind. For through the power of God and His tool of music, they have conquered timidity, overcome insecurity, and miraculously found the courage to leap tall buildings of personal challenges in a single bound.

The stories are filled with laughter. Some are filled with tears. But each one, hopefully, will inspire you to simply

see… believe…

    in miracles.

        They're all around us.

Maybe we just have to know where to

                look.

Contents

About Room 107	3
Believe	11
Christian	15
Daddy Was Once a Kid, Too	21
Ever Go to the Back of the Line?	27
Flights from Chicago	33
Goober's First Day of School	39
HUGS	45
Intelligent, Magnificent, and Spectacular	49
Just Angels	55
Ketchup	59
Little Heads Bowed	63
Maybe He's Not Mute	67
Norma Jean	73
Oh, Those Family Stories!	79
Prayer in School	85
Quiet Ones	93
R n' R	97
Sheri Learns to Tell Time	101
The Intruder	109
U Ain't S'posed to Cuss in School!	115
Very Zoe	121
When a Student Dies	127

X Husbands Come to Music 133
Yes, I Stutter. Yes, I Sing 139
Zoom In On This 145

About Room 107

What happens in this room amazes me every day. It's just an ordinary little music room, but the extraordinary always overrides its humble physical state.

You'll hear stories of children in this book. Children, who seemed selectively mute, decided they would sing and make sounds in this room. Stutterers sing solos without missing a beat. The defiant receive "heart transplants" through the miracle of God and His tool of music. I've even seen a broken foot healed.

But before I share these stories, I would first like to reveal something that I feel is the capstone, or high point to this book. It came as a surprise to me while writing one day. I discovered something about this room that I never knew. It's a God thing. And God things are miracles. So, in essence, the book's capstone is simply another miracle in my eyes. And the capstone covers all of the stories you will hear, and the stories support the capstone. What is the capstone? Well, it happens to be the number itself 107.

Here is how I discovered this "capstone." I went back to my college campus to see a room. I call it the room of negativity because it is where I, and a few more of my music major friends were discouraged about becoming music teachers.

On the first day of music theory class, our professor was twenty minutes late. He hurried through the door, slid his briefcase against the piano, threw his instrument on top, and out of breath said to us, "I don't know why you're here. Music will be out of schools by the time you graduate anyway. You'll never get a job teaching music."

And with that statement, several of my friends quit the program, got married, dropped out of school, or changed their major. A few of us were crazy enough to stick it out. I graduated with a B.S. in music education, trusting God to provide. It was scary. It was exciting.

So, as I returned to my college campus to see this room, I happened to wonder if this room, too, was number 107. It was on the first floor, the basement of the music building. I remembered that all of the rooms on that floor started in the one hundreds, of course.

As I entered the music building, I noticed the smell of the building. It still smelled the same. It smelled like any other old building. Its halls still resonated with footsteps, and conversations on all of the floors. It brought back some great memories of my college choir, and life-long friends that I made, and still have to this day. But it brought back some disturbing memories too, especially as I walked the basement hall.

I finally found the room of negativity. It was at the end of the hall, the last room on the left. It looked the same as it did when I was a freshman. For some reason, I just wanted to go in and sit in my old desk. I fancied to see how it felt to sit as a student and now as a teacher. I tried opening the door, but it was locked, so I took a picture of it instead.

As I took a picture of the door, I looked up at the number of the room. It said "103." It made me feel so good to stand before the room, knowing that God had provided not just one teaching job, He provided several teaching positions through the years after this room. I have never been without a job teaching music since I graduated.

I decided to look for Room 107. I backtracked up the hall. I passed rooms 101, 102, 103, 104, 105, and stopped at 106. Looking down the hallway of this music building, I remembered the "gloomy forecast" of music education given by several instructors in each of those rooms. And they were right. Today, music programs have been cut right and left from public education, so I can't blame them for the warning. They were just being honest. But things are not always as they appear. That's faith. And maybe faith is the most important lesson I learned in college. I thought about this while standing before room 106.

Standing there, I noticed something; the room next to it was a janitor's closet. I looked across the hall. There was another storage closet. There were no classrooms left in the hall. So, I walked down the hall again, looking for room 107. It was nowhere to be found. There was no room 107. My curiosity was put to rest. I thought to myself what a great twist it would've been for this book had the room of negativity actually been room 107, the same as my music classroom number now. I was somewhat disappointed that there was no room 107. But then the Lord reminded me of something else; something even more wonderful than the twist I wanted for my book. It was as if He spoke to my spirit and said, "Do you see the *true* miracle, Sheri?" Room 107 *is* the miracle. Rooms 101-106 were the voices of discouragement in your life saying you would never have a job teaching music. Room 107 said, "Not so."

I got in my car, and became excited with a thought! God is so into the details of my life, that He orchestrated the room numbers of my education to make a statement about his omnipotence. He ordained 107 as the capstone to my educational story. His orchestration and ordering of my steps are always nothing less than miraculous. It's that way in all of our lives as Christians. Why do we always fail to trust Him?

I called my dad, who is a pastor in North Georgia, and told him the news. He reminded me that the number seven in the Bible is the number of perfection and completion. I now see the completion of God's perfect will with the number that sits over my music classroom door. The journey to it was difficult. The journey to it was discouraging. But the journey to 107 was wonderfully miraculous.

As I was leaving my college campus, I drove around to the back of the music building. I took a picture of the room of negativity where I looked out its window daily, wondering if I was making the right decision to pursue my career as a teacher. And when I look at that picture, I still I hear the voice of my teacher echoing, "You'll never get a job, you'll never get a job." But then I think of the lyrics that I've heard in a song that says, "The voice of Truth tells me a different story."

And that's the first miracle of Room 107.

Verse of the Day:

Proverbs 3:6

"In all thy ways acknowledge him, and he shall direct thy paths."

Reflections...

How are you being discouraged in what God is calling you to do today?

What promise does Proverbs 3:6 provide for your situation today?

How can you acknowledge Christ in your words and actions today?

> "Inside every room of negativity is a window of hope. Keep looking out the window."
>
> -Sheri Thrower

Believe

The picture after this chapter is a photo of a neon sign that shines brightly over Macy's Department Store each year in New York City. It reads, "Believe."

And I ask you, "Do you believe?" More specifically, "Do you believe in miracles?"

If I took a poll, I believe that most of us would say that we believe. However, most of us probably aren't sure to what level we believe. The reason for that is that we've never seen a bona-fide true blue miracle. Or maybe we just don't know how to recognize one?

If you were to ask if I've seen a child throw down his crutches and miraculously walk around in Room 107, I would have to answer, "No," I have not seen that. "

But ask me about the parent who prayed over my broken foot to be healed. He threw down his crutches and leg braces as a child, and walked completely healed from a church altar one night after doctors told his mother he would never walk again. After his simple prayer, "God, please heal Ms. Thrower's foot," I took off my orthotic boot and ran. I still have the boot in my closet at school as a reminder that miracles happen!

If you ask me if I've seen a child raised suddenly from their bed of affliction, I would have to say, "No," to that as well. But ask me about how music can give a child dying from low self-esteem a new lease on life! I would point to the Macy's sign and say, "I believe." Yes, I've seen God use music for that miracle time after time.

I've seen a severely autistic child, who rocked back and forth, looking into space, all of sudden key in on a piano piece I was playing, only to make their way to the front of the room, slide myself off of the piano bench, and start playing the same piece in the same key, and tempo. And it was their first time to play the song. That is a miracle I've seen in Room 107. Once again, I'm pointing to the Macy's sign.

If you asked me if I've seen a blind child suddenly gain his physical sight, I would have answer, "No." But ask me if I've seen a spiritually blind teenage girl, dead to God, with a rebellious spirit, suddenly changed to see the Light of Christ through the words of a song, I would say I have seen it. That is a miracle. Salvation is always the greatest miracle.

I've seen the so-called, mute, sing. I've seen stutterers sing solos and never miss a word. I've seen the most shy, insecure children become confident and strong. I've seen a child learn to read. Those are miracles to me!

Miracles come in many shapes and sizes. It is my prayer that through the pages of this book, you will be able to put on your "miracle seeing" lenses. See the obvious, yet watch the obscure come to light. Most of all, watch how the stories of children will create a miracle within you, when you learn to believe.

I'm pointing to the Macy's sign again. Do you believe?

Verse of Day:

2 Corinthians 4:1

"So we fix our eyes not on what is seen, but on what is unseen, since what is seen is temporary, but what is seen is eternal."

"Salvation is always the greatest miracle."

Reflections...

What has God done in your life or family that you can now see as a miracle?

Since salvation is the greatest miracle, can you remember a time when you accepted this gift? If you cannot recall a time, and wish to have the gift of God's Son, Jesus, ask Him now. Thank Him for forgiveness. Share your decision with another Christian friend, or pastor.

Christian

For every so called, "difficult student," there is a teddy bear within. I really wanted to find this in my student, Christian.

Christian disrupted class sometimes, so I decided to take a different approach with him. I usually moved him to another place in the room or I would put him in time out. On this occasion, I chose to simply ignore his behavior.

I taught music classes from a cart and after Christian's class, I gathered my things and pushed my cart out the door with Christian following me to his next class.

"Hey, you can't do this you know. You aren't allowed to ignore me. I'm a student!" Christian said.

I kept walking.

"You can't do this!" he yelled.

I continued walking.

Christian finally made it to his class and I kept walking until I reached the music office. About thirty minutes later, a tanned little face with coal black curls and beautiful chocolate eyes peeped around the door.

"Hi Christian, "I said. "Whatcha need?"

"Why did you ignore me today?" he asked.

"Because I've decided to not speak to you when you're behavior is rude and disruptive in music, Christian," I said.

"I don't like that," he said.

"Yeh, I don't like it either, "I said. "What do you think needs to change?" I asked.

"Well no one likes me!" he blurted out.

"Well, I like you, Christian. I just don't like your behavior at times. And if you're having trouble making friends, maybe it's because you're not being a friend. We have to be a friend to have a friend. No one wants to hang around someone who gets into trouble all of the time, Christian," I said.

"No one likes me even when I'm nice," he said. His head drooped.

I knew Christian was a good boy beneath his tough boy exterior. I also knew he was very talented and could sing. Being in chorus would really help him gain friendships and build his self esteem, so I decided to come up with a plan to help him. I started with a colorful pencil.

"How do you like this new pencil of mine?" I asked.

"I love that pencil! It's cool. Can I have it? He asked.

I told him that he could have it only if he promised to give it to someone else. Looking at me puzzled, I said, "I want you to use this pencil as a way to be nice, Christian. As much as you like it, someone else will like it, too. When you give this pencil to someone, they will love it! So, give it to someone you like, and let me know what happens."

Christian reported back to me after giving the pencil to a sweet little girl in his classroom. He was excited to see how grateful she was. He told her that he wanted her to have it just because she was nice. I was so proud of him. He was on his way to gaining friendships.

I knew that Christian had to maintain good behavior in order to be in our chorus. The pencil plan worked. Now it was time to come up with another plan that would take place when school started back in the fall.

When school began in the fall, I spoke with his teacher and agreed to a reward system for Christian. His reward would be his choice. He chose an ice-cold coke and a pair of dress socks. I must admit, I had given plenty of cold cokes, but the dress socks were a first for me. However, that's what he wanted and that's what he would get.

Each day Christian worked diligently to get into chorus. In only a few weeks, he was loaded up on ice-cold coke, while wearing new dress socks. I was never so proud to buy nylon dress socks in all my life.

Christian joined our chorus and to my surprise, he was the most well behaved child in a group of one hundred and twenty children. Also to my surprise was how he was eager to try out for solos. I gave him a patriotic solo that he sang at the Georgia State Capitol and at our school assembly. He brought the house down at both places. When he sang at school, I was a little concerned as to how the school would respond to him. Would their reaction be positive or negative? Thankfully, their reaction was amazingly wonderful. In fact, Christian received so many high fives and hugs from his performance that it literally almost made him faint.

He came to my room and was out of breath after our chorus performance. He bent over, trying to get air. I was worried that he was hyperventilating, and asked him, "Christian, are you ok?"

He looked at me as if he was going to pass out. He took a deep breath, and with his cheek pressed against the cold cement block wall, he said, "Yes, I'm ok. But I am weak from so many hugs! I've never been hugged like that at this school. No one has ever really been nice to me until today. I feel like I'm about to pass out. Whew!"

I knew Christian was telling me the truth. His story reminds me of a saying by one of my favorite authors, Leo Buscaglia:

"Too often we underestimate the power of a touch, a smile, or a kind word, a listening ear, an honest compliment, or the smallest act of caring, all of which have the potential to turn a life around."

I, and most everyone at our school witnessed a life turned around with this little boy. I would call his moment of love and acceptance a miracle. Add another new pair of dress socks to my cart, along with an icy-cold coke!

Verse of the Day:

Zechariah 7:10

"Thus sayeth the Lord of hosts, "Render true judgment, show kindness and mercy to one another."

Reflections...

Who in your life seems difficult, needing to be softened by love? Who may need tough love?

Describe a time in your life when an act of kindness made a difference in your life.

Describe a time in your life when tough love made a difference, too.

Ask the Lord to bring someone to mind to whom you could show the love of Christ.

Do something nice for that person today.

Daddy Was Once a Kid, Too

While the following short stories did not take place in Room 107, they come from the classroom and playground of my daddy's elementary years. The Bible tells us that a merry heart is like a good medicine. So, here is some "good medicine" for your devotional moment today.

Meet my dad. He is age six in the first story. He is now seventy-four years old, and has Alzheimer's disease. I'm thankful that he still has a sense of humor. The following stories are told in his own words:

"Jimmie Lizzie Langford"

"The name of my first girlfriend when in elementary school was Jimmie Lizzie Langford. One day I wanted to call her, but I didn't know her phone number. So, I called "Information," and told the operator I wanted the phone number of "Jimmie Lizzie Langford". She searched a while in her records, but, of course, Jimmies' name wasn't there. The operator then asked me if I knew Jimmie's address. My response: "No. But she does ride bus four!"

"Smokin' in the Boy's Room"

My parents always told my siblings and me that if we ever wanted to smoke cigarettes, don't hide and do it. They told us to come tell them, and they would get the cigarettes for us to smoke.

The day came when my brother and I told them we wanted to smoke cigarettes. We were ages eight and ten. Mom went to our next-door neighbor to borrow a whole pack of cigarettes for us to smoke. They wanted us to smoke a whole pack to purposely make us sick, so we would never want to smoke again. It worked on my brother George. He got so sick he threw up everywhere. I never got sick. I enjoyed it.

Dad's next step was to make me feel guilty for smoking cigarettes. He put a stool in front of a mirror, and told me, "Come here boy. Stand on this stool. Look in this mirror to see how bad you look smoking cigarettes!"

As I stood on the stool to watch myself blow cigarette smoke into the air, my dad, hoping to shame me from ever smoking again, said, "Well Boy, how do you think you *now*, smoking those cigarettes"?

As I watched the smoke coming out my mouth, encircling the room, I responded, "I look great dad!"

His next step, hoping to correct me even more from ever smoking cigarettes again, was to let me know what Jesus thought about it.

In his low preacher's voice he said, "What do you think Jesus thinks as He watches you smoking these sinful cigarettes? Don't you think you need to ask Jesus to forgive you for smoking, and promise Him you will never do it again"?

I had no choice but to tearfully responded with, "yes."

Dad and I got on our knees together, and I asked Jesus to forgive me for smoking. (I should insert here that smoking, going to movies, and women wearing sleeveless dresses to church were all considered "sins" when I was a boy. Times have changed since then.)

Soon after that, Dad was called to be pastor of his first prestigious church, "The First Baptist Church," in Moore Haven, Florida. Our dad previously pastored of a country church Palma Sola, Florida. It was so small, that he picked up his entire congregation for church in our car.

On his first Wednesday night at First Baptist, dad asked the congregation if anyone wanted to give a testimony of how Jesus did something good for them.

I, the third grade son of the new pastor, immediately stood up from my pew and said, "Yes daddy, I have something to say. I want to thank the Lord for saving my soul, and rescuing me from a Devil's hell."

You could hear "Amen!" resound all over the congregation.

I continued. "I also want to thank Him for delivering me from the cigarette smoking habit!"

Daddy's congregation looked at me with shock and horror. My mother slowly sank down in her seat, wanting to "crawl under the pew." You could hear snickers and giggles from most of the audience, but I'm sure some wondered if they had made the right decision to hire a pastor whose eight year old son was delivered from "nicotine addiction."

Not too long after that, while I was in another room of our home, I heard my father say to my mother, "I would love to give the congregation more opportunities to give their testimony of how the Lord has been good to them. But I know *that boy* is going to give *that same* testimony of how God delivered him from the smoking habit!"

I love stories like this from my parent's childhood. Isn't it interesting how times have changed? I let a young fourteen-year-old writer from my writing class read this story. She was stunned that smoking was considered a sin when my dad was a boy. Most teens these days have a hard time believing that television was wrong in some households. Going to movies, and wearing pants were also considered sins, too. My mom informed me just this week that sleeveless dresses worn to church were definitely a "no-no" in her day.

While the story of my dad as a preacher's kid may seem extreme, I feel it has an important spiritual message. While my grandfather used extreme measures to keep my dad and his brothers from smoking, and while it may have seemed a bit harsh, it was effective. Are extreme measures like this too harsh? As an educator, seeing the devastating effects of drugs and alcoholism in the lives of youth today, I must say that I think we sometimes need extreme measures, even fear tactics, to save a life.

The flip side of that is that the Bible speaks about the goodness of God leading us to repentance. I've seen the hardest heart softened by the goodness of God. However, what I'm seeing in today's classroom is that it's almost like we're living in an overload of sugary sweet grace. We can be guilty of sprinkling grace over every unhealthy life style, and hope for the best. The fear of God can be a good thing.

God's word says something interesting about this in Jude 1 where it says, "**22**Be merciful to those who doubt; **23**save others by snatching them from the fire; to others show mercy, mixed with fear—hating even the clothing stained by corrupted flesh."

God says it's important to use both. Show mercy. To others, snatch them! We have to do both.

The fear of the Lord is a good thing. And it's something rare to find in youth today. We can be kind and diplomatic, and that may be effective. But healthy fear can be a good thing.

Could it be that my grandfather's tactic snatched my dad from something that would've been detrimental to his health, and ultimately, his witness a Christian? My dad is a minister of the gospel today and so is his brother. I will have to say that they are two of the finest men I know.

Thanks to a whole lot of love and a little bit of snatching.

Verse of the Day:

Proverbs 17:22
"A merry heart doeth good *like* a medicine: but a broken spirit drieth the bones." KJV

Proverbs 1:7

"The fear of the LORD is the beginning of knowledge, but fools despise wisdom and instruction."

Reflections...

How has The Lord used laughter to get you through some tough times?

How has the fear of the Lord been used as a positive influence in your life?

Ever Go to the Back of the Line?

A common saying of teachers is, "Go to the back of the line." Excessive talkers, class clowns, troublemakers, and runners find themselves at the back of the line when they've been disobedient, or making the teacher feel like pulling her hair out at the end of the day.

I woke up from my sleep at 3 a.m. one morning with the phrase, "Can't go back" in my head. How many times have I felt like I've been sent to "the back of the line" in my life? At times, I've felt like God has given me "the look" that I've seen my earthly father give me from the pulpit when I acting up in church. It's as if He's pointing his long, judgmental finger at me, motioning me to take the long trip down the hallway of where I've been, to stand and think about my actions. It's as if He's saying, "Walk it again, sistah." As a teacher, I've sent children to the back of the line, as they have raced down the hall to my room. "To the back, and walk please.

God's long judgmental finger is an image of our making. That image is not God at all. God does discipline us. He guides us with a loving eye and hand. Yet, He is firm. Have you ever been there? You've made the same mistakes in life over and over? It could be another failed relationship, another burst of your temper, another vomiting of hurtful words on someone you love-the list goes on and on. And you find yourself repeating those situations. It's as if God is saying, "Try it again. Go back to the end of the line. Let's get it right." God wants us to get it right in order to protect us. His correction in our lives is always motivated by love.

I call it God's school house of correction. God, as our teacher, sends us back down the hallways of where we've made mistakes in order to bring us down the hall again; this time, doing it a different way. Getting hurt over and over in a relationship because of wrong decisions can do that. "Go back to the end of the line, please." Saying hurtful words or losing our tempers can do that. "Go back to the end of the line, please." Making poor decisions with our finances can send us to the end of the line, too. "Go back…" You get the picture. God has a better plan.

The children of Israel knew this all too well. They were sent to the back of the line about forty times, as they complained about God down the hallway of deliverance. "Manna again this morning?" "Go to the…" you can finish the sentence. Israel stayed in the wilderness forty years when they could've been at the Promised Land in only 8 days. The back of the line can cost us years.

The alcoholic or drug addict understands this. Each time they put their addiction above their families, intimacy in their relationships with family members takes steps back to the end of the line. People who commit adultery know it all too well. Selfish unfaithfulness repeatedly shattering the hearts of all family members like a glass vase smashed on the ground, sends them to the back of the line. They are far from the trust of their children, spouses, and friends.

God sends us to the back of the line out of His mercy and love. Mercy allows us God's discipline. Mercy allows us to be sent back to "do things over again" because God is giving us a second chance. In many cases, God gives us a third, fourth, and fiftieth chance. It's His way of saying, "Try it again. You can do it."

If you've been sent to the back of the line this week in your life, know that God in His mercy has taken you there. It's your chance to try it one more time. It's your chance to follow Him one more time. It's your chance to watch the faithful walking in front of you, leading by example. Walk behind the faithful and follow.

Once we learn the lesson God has for us in one place, He takes us further up the hallway to a new place in Him.

In God's word for today, The Lord allowed two people to follow Him into the Promised Land because of their obedience. They were at the head of line, so to speak: Numbers 32:10-12 tells of this as it says, 10"The Lord's anger was aroused that day and he swore this oath: 11'Because they have not followed me wholeheartedly, not one of those who were twenty years old or more when they came up out of Egypt will see the land I promised on oath to Abraham, Isaac and Jacob— 12not one except Caleb son of Jephunneh the Kenizzite and Joshua son of Nun, for they followed the Lord wholeheartedly."

I love how this verse says, "Not one of them," and then it adds the word, "except." Exceptions are made for those who not only follow the Lord, but follow Him wholeheartedly.

Are you following Him wholeheartedly today? Is there an area of your life that is keeping you from seeing your promised land? Thank the Lord for loving you enough to keep it from you until you follow Him wholeheartedly. Will it be easy? No. Will it cost you something? Yes; your obedience, and your comfort. Will you have set backs? Maybe. But once you choose to follow Him, your promised land will be worth it.

Do you want to go?

Verse of the Day:

Joshua 1:13

"Remember the word that Moses the servant of the Lord commanded you, saying, 'The Lord your God is providing you a place of rest and will give you this land.'

Reflections...

Have you ever felt like you have been sent to the back of the line in your life? If so, what areas of your life do you find a challenge to be obedient?

In your own words, tell the Lord you wish to surrender that part of your life today:

What does He say in His word about your situation?

Read Numbers 32. What is God saying to you through His word? What can you do today to follow the Lord in this area?

Flights from Chicago

"Billy," as I'll refer to him in this story, was a quiet little boy. He was solemn and never said a word in music class. He had brown sugar skin, with beautiful waves and curls, and light green eyes that could melt twenty feet of winter snow. He was an angel of a child, and I wish I had a hundred like him. He was obedient to the tenth power.

One day while in the middle of teaching, quiet little Billy raised his hand to speak. It was unusual for him to speak at all, much less raise his hand to interrupt instructional time. So, afraid he was sick, or about to throw up, I stopped to notice him.

"Yes, Billy?" I said with concern.

Billy slowly rose to his feet, paused, looked around the room, looked at me, and said, "Ms. Thrower, I love this class so much."

Obviously, Billy was not sick. And with concern in my voice, I answered, "Well, thank you very much, Billy."

I started to kindly ask him to have a seat, but as I got the first syllable out of my mouth, he boldly interrupted, "…And…and…I take a flight from Chicago to come to this music class every Tuesday!"

Stunned and not knowing what got into Billy, I replied, "Well. Billy. That is very kind of you. I'm glad you love music class so much that you would fly in to be with us. Thank you! And I hope your flight is on time today, and the next time you fly to be with us next week."

With the most solemn look on his face, he paused looking at me, and without blinking an eye, whispered, "Thank you, ma'am."

And with that, Billy sat down.

This has to be one of the most memorable moments of my teaching career. It also has to be the most difficult time I've ever had trying not to burst into a gut-busting belly laugh. I just could not hurt his feelings by laughing at his sincere love for music, as far-fetched as his story was.

And I wonder. Do I show my love for Jesus as much as Billy showed his love for music? In Billy's mind, he was willing to take a plane and travel from Chicago just for his love of music. And I take the shortest, most convenient ways to Jesus and His ways. Forget a plane to His will. I've been guilty of building my own rocket ships made of my self-will. I have jumped into time capsules of my own making, and placed myself light years ahead of His will and His plan. Oh, I've flown alright. I've flown straight into huge, big messes. And I've flown ninety to nothing straight into it.

Maybe you can relate. You are flying into things you know you should not even go near. It could be a relationship you know is not God's will for your life. It could be a financial decision. It could be a job you know is not right. It could be many things. Maybe it's something that only you and God know about.

God's word has much to say about where we go, and what we spend our time doing. He has much to say about the flight you're on today, and where you are headed. We don't need to rush into things that He's warning us about. But we do need to rush, or "Take the flight" to where He's leading. And sometimes He leads us to a place of rest. And He's serious about taking that flight, and getting there fast.

Just as we labor at an airport to board our destinations when flying, rushing through customs, checking our luggage, hurrying to get to our gate; God wants us to labor, hurry, and "get to" His Sabbath, His place of rest. Why? He wants us to rest because we are worn out from doing things our way. We are worn out from sin, and its consequences. Sometimes, we are simply worn out from life. He wants you to rest.

Hebrews 4:11 says, "Let us therefore make every effort to enter that rest, so that no one will perish by following their example of disobedience." (NIV)

Today, consider the Word of God for your life. Make every effort to enter that rest. Take the next flight to the land of rest of stay there until God tells you to move.

For me, as I'm writing this, God has put me on the red eye flight to His place of rest. I have been sick with bronchitis, and swollen vocal chords for one week. I can't talk, I can't sing, I can't teach. It has come at an appropriate time, during our fall break at school. God knew when to knock me off my feet in silence. He knew the flight I needed to the land of rest. I am resting. I am praying. I am writing. I'm thankful for His rest. Psalm 23 says it best in verse 2: "He makes me lie down in green pastures…"

A place of rest, that's a flight worth going to.

Verse of the Day:

Psalm 23:1-2

"The Lord is my Shepherd, I shall not want. He makes me to lie down in green pastures…"

Reflections...

From what situation is God calling you to rest?

What steps can you take today to "take the next flight" and get away from your distractions?

Describe your place of rest. Pray and ask God to lead you the rest in His will.

Goober's First Day of School

It was kindergarten's first day of music. I always make the children feel welcome by singing their name. After I sing their name, I have the children join me in clapping their name. Sometimes we pat their name on our laps, on the floor, on our heads, etc. It's fun sounding out each child's name, and watching their reaction.

I had sung almost everyone in the room's name, except for one last boy. I said, "What is your name, honey?"

He said, "Goober."

I have to admit, this is the very first child named Goober I had ever taught. I also have to admit that at that moment, I wondered why his mom gave him that name. But at any rate, I wanted Goober to feel special, so we sang his name, clapped it, raised the roof with it, and more. I had a little extra time left until their teacher came, so I took a little more time with Goober's name. We "drove the truck," "bounced the pretend basketball," and more while chanting, "GOO-ber, GOO-ber!"

After a few more songs, it was time for the class to go back to their homeroom. Their teacher showed up at the door to get her class, and they all ran to get in line. As they were exiting my room, I made a special point to give each one a high five or a pat on the head, and thank them for coming to music.

Goober was last in line on the way out. He approached me at the door, and I said, "Goober, I'm so glad you came to music today! I hope you've had a great time."

Goober looked up at me so confused and said, "My name is COO-per!"

Ok. I felt like a heel for calling this child the wrong name. I could envision him in high school one day with a bunch of kids around him saying, "Hey, Goob! Remember when Ms. Thrower called you Goober in music class? And that's how you got your name?"

I could just imagine the laughter that would echo down the halls of that school because of me calling this child the wrong name. I could also imagine him on a psychiatrist's couch one day saying, "It all started with my music teacher on the first day of school…"

To make things a little better for Cooper, a.k.a, Goober, I made a special effort to take him candy as I walked past his homeroom each day that week. I stopped in to see him and made sure I pronounced his name correctly.

I would stick my head in the door and say, "Just checking to see how my friend, COO-per is doing today!"

I would see Cooper, and give him a thumb's up. He would smile really big. The whole time I was giving him a thumb's up, I was thinking, "Please don't tell your mother what I did!"

Well, the first week came and went, and I finally met Cooper's mommy. I didn't know if I should tell her my real name, or make up a name. If I told her my real name, "Ms. Thrower," she would probably punch me in the nose for harming her child's self-image for life.

I decided to play it safe, so I said, "Hello, you must be Cooper's mother?"

She said, "Yes, I am."

I said, "Well, I just love having COOOOOOO-per in music class! (I made sure to emphasize, "COO" in his name.)

Then I continued, "Has he had a great first week of school?"

After that question flew out of my mouth, I knew I had opened myself up for a double barrel. Fortunately, she did not pull out a rifle and chase me around the room nor try to kill me with a frying pan.

She said, "Oh he just loved the first week of school! And he loves music class. He comes home singing every song you teach the class."

I gave her a "thumbs up," wiped the sweat from my brow and exited from Cooper's classroom. Thank the Lord, Cooper liked music, and his mom did not kill me for calling him, "Goober." I think that is a miracle!

Verse of the Day:

Proverbs 22:1

"A good name is more desirable than great riches; to be esteemed is better than silver or gold."

Reflections...

While the story of "Goober" was written in a lighthearted manner, being labeled wrongly or negatively is no laughing matter. What names/labels have been placed on you that have hurt?

What does scripture say about you in the following verse?

2 Corinthians 5:21

"[21] He made the One who did not know sin to be sin[a] for us, so that we might become the righteousness of God in Him."

I am the _____ of _____ in Him.

As a parent, it is important to call our children names that are uplifting. "Lazy, silly, no good-just-like-your-father/mother," are a few examples of names that produce poor self-image. Ask God to remind you daily about your children's best qualities. As He reminds you, make a special effort to tell them. Send them a text reminding them of their wonderful-ness! Ask their forgiveness if you've called them hurtful names.

"To Be Fully Seen By Someone And Then Loved Anyhow- That Is A Human Offering That Can Border On Miraculous."

-Elizabeth Gilbert

HUGS

Children are huggers. Have you ever noticed? When a child loves someone, they hug. And they hug a lot.

I wish that I had a dollar for every morning that a child opens the door of my music room, steps in with their arms extended, to hug me. Sometimes they never say a word. They just give me that look that says, "So glad to see you," walk to my desk, wrap their little arms around me, smile, and then skip back to class.

Children teach me to love. They teach us all to love. And I ask myself the question: How many mornings do I open the door to God's presence, and give him a hug? How many times do I start off my morning with a spiritual hug? Do I even know how?

We think our approach to God has to be so formal. My children at school never open my door with, "Oh thou most wonderful Ms. Thrower. I boldly come into your classroom today, giving you hugs and praise for being our great teacher. I come to extend my arms to you this morning as a token of my many thanks. May your day be blessed and full of grace. Amen."

No. My children open the door of my room and may not even say a word. Some may say, "See ya!" as they pass by.

Others simply step in to make their presence known and give a hug. That's how we approach God. It's not as difficult as we think. He is approachable.

The next time you wake up to begin your day, try making your presence known to God with your affection. You may say something as simple as, "Good morning, Lord." You could even talk further with Him, telling Him how you need Him for your day. "God, I need you today, in every way." He just wants us to talk to Him. You may start off your day by giving him a thankful hug, "Lord, thank you for another day to be alive."

Open the door. Step into His presence. Give him a Him a hug with your thanks and praise.

Verse of the Day:

Psalm 100:4, "Enter his gates with thanksgiving and his courts with praise; give thanks to him and praise his name."

Reflections...

Give Jesus your best hug by thanking Him for five blessings in your life:

What short phrase can you say to Him right now that is sincere and from your heart?

For what are you most thankful? Tell Him.

Tell Him how thankful you are for His cross and your salvation:

Intelligent, Magnificent, and Spectacular

Kindergarten vocabulary has grown over the years. The words are longer than the length of their little bodies it seems. Here's what I mean:

On one particular day, a group of kindergarteners hit my classroom. I say they hit the classroom, because that's the only way kindergarteners enter any room. They hit the scene.

The first group of children to come for music was led by one little spunky guy who looked at me, and said, "Well, well, Ms. Froher, don't you look so *intelligent* wearing those glasses today?"

I did have on a brand new pair of reading glasses, and thought they must look ok if the kids say so. The saying is true that kids are honest.

The next five came in, "Ms. Froher, your outfit is *magnificent* today!"

I had on sweat pants. It was dress down day, but what the heck, I thought. Maybe my sweat pants weren't as worn looking as I thought. The kids would tell me, right?

The last of the caravan came in the door and a little one shouted, "Hey, Ms. Froher! You are a *spectacular* music teacher today!"

Wow! I felt great after all of those generous compliments. I felt like I could do anything (Insert picture here of me wearing a big "S" on my shirt, with a red cape and bright blue tights. Yes, I'm flexing my muscles).

I taught that class with so much zeal. I think I was kinder that day, too. I even thought about rewarding them and taking them out for extra time on the playground due to their generous compliments.

Finally, music time ended, and they all lined up. Then their homeroom teacher peaked her head in the door and said, "Have the kids shared their vocabulary words with you today, Ms. Thrower? What are our vocabulary words for the day, boys and girls?"

In unison, the class said together, "Intelligeeeent, Magnificeeeeeent, and Spectaaaaaclur!" Twenty-six toothless smiles, and three huge new vocabulary words marched out of music class that day, and I was left speechless from the reality that they weren't really talking about me at all. However, three words changed the atmosphere of my room that day. It's amazing what a positive vocabulary can do. I felt intelligent. I felt magnificent. I felt spectacular. I felt energized. Words can do that.

We hear much about our words to each other, which is important, but what about our words to God? Let's look at what our words can do.

Psalm 91

"I will say of the LORD, "He is my refuge and my fortress,
  my God, in whom I trust."

³ Surely he will save you
  from the fowler's snare
  and from the deadly pestilence.
⁴ He will cover you with his feathers,
  and under his wings you will find refuge;

his faithfulness will be your shield and rampart.
⁵ You will not fear the terror of night,
  nor the arrow that flies by day,
⁶ nor the pestilence that stalks in the darkness,
  nor the plague that destroys at midday.
⁷ A thousand may fall at your side,
  ten thousand at your right hand,
  but it will not come near you.
⁸ You will only observe with your eyes
  and see the punishment of the wicked.

⁹ If you say, "The LORD is my refuge,"
  and you make the Most High your dwelling,
¹⁰ no harm will overtake you,
  no disaster will come near your tent.
¹¹ For he will command his angels concerning you
  to guard you in all your ways;
¹² they will lift you up in their hands,
  so that you will not strike your foot against a stone.
¹³ You will tread on the lion and the cobra;
  you will trample the great lion and the serpent."

Psalm 91 promises us protection and provision, but it is contingent upon what we say of the Lord. In other words, we say, and then He does. His actions are a direct result of our declaration of Him.

There are some key words in this chapter that we should add to our vocabulary when talking with God. The next time you approach His presence, carry the Psalm 91 vocabulary with you just like the kids brought their new vocabulary room 107. Enter His presence with: "Lord, you are my *refuge* today. And Lord, I'm so glad you are my *fortress,* too. You are the biggest word I can think of. That word is *God.* You are God over my situation.

Did you say it? There, you just changed the atmosphere of your circumstances. You said some great things about your God. Now watch Him do great things for you.

Verse of the Day:

Psalm 91

Reflections...

What has the tone of your conversation been lately regarding your life situations and circumstances?

Take the next twenty-four hours and tell God how great He is. Lay aside the negativity and what ifs of the day, and focus on your spiritual vocabulary. "Say of the Lord" in the space below:

After twenty-four hours of the above exercise, how has your circumstances changed? How have you changed in your approach to talking and praying to God?

Miracles In Room 107

King of Kings

Savior

Wonderful Counselor

Provider

Deliverer

Lord of Lords

Friend

Just Angels

There's a framed picture of my daughter, Averi, on top of the piano in room 107. It reminds me of a country song that says, "I believe there are angels among us…"

I do believe in angels. One reason is because of my little girl in the frame. When she was only two, she "saw" and "talked" to an angel in our house.

Our family was watching television one night when it suddenly turned off. It wasn't storming, so that was not the reason for the outage. It just turned off. When this happened, Averi looked around me to the rocking chair where her dad was sitting. She waved her little hands, as if to say, 'hello" to someone. She was not looking at her dad; she was looking past him.

She then put her little index finger up to her mouth, as if to say, "Ok, I won't tell," making a hush sign.

She smiled and grinned a lot at something. We had no idea what was going on. We just assumed it was her little imagination.

Suddenly, her dad got out of his recliner, and he went down the hall. He came back and went into the kitchen.

Averi looked at me and said, "Where is daddy's angel? Where did daddy's angel go?"

I wondered how she even knew the word, "angel," much less be talking about one at her age. And *seeing* one? *Talking* to one? I summed it up as her imagination.

It was time for Averi to go to bed, so her dad and I took her into her room. I was holding her, then she started giggling. She started the waving motions again with her hand and was obviously communicating with something we couldn't see.

She put her little index finger up to her mouth again, nodded her head in a "yes motion," and said, "Ok. Shhhhhh. "

She got in her bed and peacefully went to sleep.

Later that night, around midnight, when her dad and I were sound asleep, we heard the sound of three chimes. It awakened both of us. I turned to my husband and said, "Did you hear that?"

He told me he did. When I turned to ask him if he heard the three chimes, I saw a tall figure in white at his side. It was a soldier-like figure, tall, and carrying a shield, and dressed in armor head to toe.

I told him, "You know the angel Averi has been talking to? I see it now. It's right beside you. Can you see it?"

I could see a very tall protective figure beside our bed, and I was not afraid. The figure faded into the dark of the night. I feel sure the Lord let me see what my little girl had seen earlier. It was our protective angel.

Matthew 18:10 tells about children and angels where it says: "See to it that you do not despise one of these little ones, because I tell you, their angels in heaven always have access to my Father in heaven."

Notice that the verse says, *"their angels."* Children must have angels. When I read that verse, I can see why God gave angels to children. How else can you explain eating bugs, spiders, dirt, and not croaking over? Angels to the rescue!

I believe children have protection at school, too. As an educator, I see more children stressed out over broken home situations. I'm sure their angels are on "comforting patrol" twenty-four-seven. I've always admired the tenacity of children. They amaze me at the way they come to school and do their work in the midst of domestic chaos and trauma in their little worlds. It's amazing that children can do well on state test scores when their minds and hearts are overwhelmed with family problems. There have been many times while I've been teaching music that a little one will raise their hand and say, "I miss my dad. He left last night." I can imagine that child's angel placing its wings around them at that very moment. Children need angels.

I've said it once, and I'll say it again in this book, it is humorous to me when I hear that God is no longer in our schools. Are you kidding me? Not only is God in our schools, but I bet an army of angels is there, too. We just don't see them.

Well, most of us don't.

But there's that little girl in the frame…

Verse of the Day:

Hebrews 1:14

"Are not all angels ministering spirits sent to serve those who will inherit salvation?

Reflections...

Has there been a time when you felt God sent angelic assistance to you? Describe.

If you could ask for angelic assistance in your life, in what area would you need it?

What are you afraid of most?

Pray and ask God to send His angels, His ministering spirits on your behalf.

Ketchup

Some days, it's a miracle if you make it through the day all in one piece. On this particular day, someone's hot dog lost its ketchup. And I found it.

The lunchroom was so noisy that day. I kept thinking to myself, "If I can just slip away from this noise and eat."

I slipped away, all right. I got my tray and made my way across the lunchroom floor. I slipped, and before I could catch myself, I fell slowly, doing the splits into a pile of ketchup on the lunchroom floor. It seemed like a slow motion movie. I could see everyone's head turning, and slowly in unison saying, "Ohhhh noooooooo."

You could hear the whole cafeteria gasp as I hit the floor, and painted my clothes in red from the puddle beneath me. Don't get me wrong. One of my colors *is* red. However, the fragrance of dried ketchup after a long day is not my fragrance of the day.

I laughed it off. The PE teacher and I busted our guts laughing, and it really brought some stress relief to my day, believe it or not. In fact, I think "Ms. Froher" brought some unexpected stress relief to the entire cafeteria that day. I'm glad that I "could be a blessin."

It matters where we walk. As Christians, God's word tells us to be wise. Sometimes we hurry off into the ketchup, or slippery places in life. I've done it. You've done it, too. It's called, "Doing what we want." We head towards things that we have no business heading to. Sometimes we don't see the slippery places while walking. We just stumble across them like spilled ketchup on the floor. And once we've fallen in those places, we get up smelling like where we've been.

The good news is that God orders our steps in His word. When we walk in relationship with Christ, we walk with Him. He walks with us. When we get away from Him, it's like ketchup on the floor.

Verse of the Day:

Ephesians 5:15

"Therefore be careful how you walk, not as unwise men but as wise…"

Reflections...

Where are the slippery places you've been walking?

Read your bible. Where is God leading you to walk? What verse has He given you to confirm this?

Little Heads Bowed

I'm amazed how God works, especially when it's in the middle of writing a book, and I forget to write a chapter!

My chapters are in alphabetical order, and chapter "L" had not yet been written. I had no idea what to write. But then, yesterday happened.

I was teaching music to a fifth grade class when my cell phone sounded. I had a text. We're not supposed to use our phones in class, but today, I was expecting important news from my sister. Her doctor's appointment was today. She had received a questionable mammogram, and today she would find out if it was cancer.

I stopped teaching, walked over to my cell phone, picked it up and read: "We'll know something in 40 minutes." I froze and just looked straight ahead.

Silence fell over my class as the children were looking at me with concern. I decided to be honest with them.

I looked at them and said, "I know that we aren't supposed to use cell phones in class, boys and girls, but I just got a text from my mom that is very important. My sister is having tests today to see if she has cancer, and I want to make sure she's ok." I told them that I would know something in forty minutes. I also looked at them and said, "You know I can't ask you all to pray because we are in school. But if you think about it sometime after music, and you want to, please think of my sister, and pray for her if you believe in prayer. I would never push prayer on anyone, so only if you want to."

My class looked around at each other and one by one, every child in my class bowed their head and had a moment of silence. Not one word was said. However, I know there were precious silent words of petition that went straight to the ears of our Heavenly Father. I know He heard their prayer and it was as incense before his throne.

My class left, and forty minutes passed. I got a phone call from my mom saying all was well. No cancer. I thank God my sister was spared.

Later that day, several of my students dropped by room 107 and said, "Have you heard about your sister yet, Ms. Thrower?" I was so glad to tell them that she was ok and that God heard their prayers!

Later that morning I stopped by the fifth graders' room that prayed in my room when I got the text. I poked my head in their door and said, "I just want you all to know that my sister is just fine. Thank you for praying!" They smiled. I hope they will always remember the time God heard their prayer.

A seed was planted today. A chapter was written today. Encouragement was birthed into the lives of about twenty-six children, who may want to see if God answers more prayers down the road.

I'm thankful for the miracle of little bowed heads in room 107.

Verse of the Day

Isaiah 65:2

"Before they call I will answer; while they are still speaking I will hear."

Reflections...

Write a prayer to God, asking Him to meet your greatest need today.

Thank Him that He has heard you and has already answered.

Maybe He's Not Mute

It was kindergarten's first day of music when the cutest little boy entered my room. He smiled with his lips closed. His big brown eyes looked around my music room with wonder.

His para-pro whispered to me, "This little boy doesn't talk, Ms. Thrower. He won't be singing in music. Just thought you needed to know. He doesn't talk at *all.*" She smiled and left.

I gathered the children around to teach them some fun songs. I love teaching them the song, "This Land is Your Land." They love the song, and it is a great song to add sound effects to. I decided that after teaching them the words, I would teach them to sing the song with different animal sounds.

I said, "Who can sing the song like a dog barking?" They loved barking the song. I looked at my new little quiet friend, and he was barking away, too. He loved music.

After singing the song, I asked the children to tell me their names. When I got to this little boy, the children blurted out, "He can't tell you his name. He doesn't talk."

To which I replied, "Oh yes, he does." Then looking at the little boy, I said, "Don'tcha bud?" He quickly shifted his eyes to another part of the room. I wondered if he was selectively mute, but I didn't wish to label him.

A few months went by and his story had not changed. He still wasn't talking. But I couldn't help to think it was funny that he was still singing.

Christmas approached, and I knew this little boy was going to love our Christmas songs. I knew that the chorus of "Jingle Bells" would be a fun song and easy for him to sing. He would move his little mouth to the chorus as best as he could.

After Christmas, I found out that his mommy had a baby. Several of the children in his room had new baby brothers and sisters for Christmas. Santa brought babies to their tree!

I decided to ask this little boy about his new baby. I looked at him and asked, "If I guess the letter that your new baby's name starts with, will you let me know if I'm right?"

He shook his head, "yes."

I said, "Well, is it a girl or a boy?"

He held up two fingers. I assumed that he meant the second choice was correct, so I said, "The second one? It's a baby brother?" He nodded his head, "yes."

I wanted so badly for this little boy to talk to me! So, I decided to make up funny names for his baby brother, if I could guess the letter it started with.

I said, "Does his name start with an A?"

He shook his head, "no."

I said, "Does his name start with a B?"

He shook his head, "yes."

"Your baby brother's name starts with a B? Yay! I guessed it! Oh, if I could just guess his name. Is his name Barney?"

He looked at me and shouted out, "No!"

The class gasped, and shouted, "He can talk!"

I said, "Of course, he can talk. Can't you, sweetie?"

He shifted his eyes to the side.

I continued to ask him about his brother. Is his name, "Bartholomew?"

Disgusted at that name, he yelled, "Noooooo!"

"Oh, Ok." I said.

"Hmmm...what about Braden? Is his name Braden?"

He said, "Yes!"

To which I replied, "Yay! His brother's name is Braden, everyone! Let's sing Braden's name!" So we all sang, "Braden" to the tune of "This Land is Your Land." My little friend was so happy to sing his brother's name. He threw his head back and sang it loud and proud.

There have been many times when I have just wanted to throw my arms around this little boy and beg God to help him speak. I have prayed many times for him in the privacy of my home.

He moved later in the year and I don't know if I'll ever see him again. His homeroom teacher and others worked wonders with him as they helped him to say his vowel sounds and count. We all miss him. I hope he keeps singing and keeps making progress wherever he is. The memory of him in my class only reminds me that I'm so thankful for the many ways God uses education and music to touch lives. It seems miraculous.

Verse of the Day

Psalm 139: 4

"For there is not a word in my tongue (still unuttered), but, behold, O Lord, You know it altogether."

Reflections...

What physical or emotional mountain is in your life today?

Has it kept you from talking to God? How long?

Take a step of faith and talk to The Lord. Start by telling Him that you love Him. Thank Him for something good that has happened to you today or this week.

Norma Jean

I'm turning back the hands of time on this story. Come with me to my first grade class.

When you like to laugh, there are just some people you don't need to sit near in class. For me, that person was Cindy. She and I got in so much trouble for giggling and talking in class. When we were separate we were model students. But together we were Lucy and Ethel.

Cindy and I were not at all like Norma Jean. Her behavior was as perfect as her neatly trimmed bangs. She towered over the rest of us with her beautiful, ruler straight posture. She wore a bowl hair cut with what I call first grade bangs. If you're a woman, I bet you had them, too. First grade bangs are bangs that looked like our moms trimmed them with a professional Troy Built hedge trimmer. Cindy had them, I had them, and so did Norma Jean. And that's about the only thing we shared in common.

Norma Jean was quiet, mostly serious, and didn't smile much. She was very shy and you could tell that even walking in front of the class to sharpen her pencil was embarrassing to her. If you looked up the word "insecure" in the dictionary, you would probably see Norma Jean's first grade picture. On the other hand, Cindy and I were poster children for "Pranksters R Us." We decided to do our friend a favor, and to loosen her up a bit!

Norma did not like being called on to talk or answer questions in front of the class. But there was this one time in math…

As in every math block, our teacher would present the class with a math problem, and we would raise our hands to give the solution. Her first question of the day: "Can anyone tell me what ten plus ten is?"

I guess we were just learning to count with two digit numbers, and that was a challenging question for us. While everyone was counting their fingers and throwing off their socks to count their toes for the answer, I decided to have some fun with Norma.

I mouthed to Cindy, "Watch this!" I leaned over my desk and whispered in Norma Jean's ear, "Do you know the answer to ten plus ten, Norma Jean?"

She whispered back to me, "No. Do you?"

"Yes!" I said. "The answer is two thousand, five hundred, Norma Jean. Stand up and tell the teacher!"

I'd like to pause here and say that my mischievousness was soon paid back as you will later read at the end of this chapter. I'd also like to say that my dad is a preacher, and you've heard stories about how preacher's kids are. My excuse for being a mischievous preacher's kid is due to the fact that I played with the deacon's kids. Enough said. Moving on with the story now.

Norma Jean turned and looked confused by my answer to the math problem. I winked at Cindy and whispered, "Isn't ten plus ten two thousand, five hundred, Cindy?"

Cindy jumped right in on my prank. "Yes, it is! Ten plus ten is two thousand, five hundred, Norma Jean. Tell the teacher!"

Norma Jean stood up and my heart sank to the bottom of the hard wood floor below me. The first thought that came to me was, "My mother would have my rear end if she knew about this. Oh well, she'll never find out." (My apologies mom, if you're reading this!)

The teacher called on Norma Jean. "Yes, Norma Jean? What is ten plus ten?" Norma Jean, arms tight and straight against her body, took a deep breath, cleared her throat, and said, "Ten plus ten is two thousand five...." And before she could finish her answer, our teacher rolled her eyes and said, "Sit *down*, Norma Jean."

Cindy and I were in trouble.

It probably comes as no surprise to you that Cindy and I were separated for the rest of the year after that incident. And you're probably wondering about the spiritual application of this story.

All I know is that I learned at an early age that we reap what we sow. And I have the class picture to prove it!

Although payback time was a few years later, it happened when my mom took me to get my hair trimmed. My hair was long, reaching the middle of my back and I wanted to keep it that way. I explained to the hairdresser that I just wanted a trim. However, she was new to her profession and got scissor happy. I sat in her beauty parlor chair with a black apron covering my shoulders and watched as inches of my hair fell like autumn leaves to the linoleum floor below. Chop, chop, chop! My hair ended up short, just below my ears and framed with "First grade bangs." I felt like I was in first grade all over again.

After the hairdresser was done cutting my hair, she asked me to sit in the lobby and wait for my mother, who was going to pick me up after running a few errands. My mother came in, sat down beside me, looked straight ahead, and said nothing.

Finally, I said, "Mom, she cut off all of my hair." I started to cry.

My mom gasped, and said, "Oh my goodness, I didn't know that was you sitting beside me! What happened?" I knew exactly what happened. I spent the rest of the school year learning what Norma Jean must have felt in first grade. Humiliation is not a fun lesson. But it was an important lesson none the less.

I learned that there are some life lessons we learn from our parents. And there are some life lessons we learn from God Himself. God can teach a lesson like no one else. In fact, I remember as a teen going through a time of challenging my parents a bit in my teen years, and my dad saying to me, "Alright, if you're not going to listen to me and your mother, we're turning you over to the Lord. His discipline will be more effective anyway." He was right! And I think that my hair cut was used as His new lesson to teach me compassion. Maybe the miracle of this story is when we finally "get it" that God is loving, but He also teaches us life lessons that are difficult sometimes. It's called tough love.

As a parent, I would like to encourage you to trust God with His lessons in your own child's life. Even if the lessons may seem hard, let Him do a work that only He can do. God is merciful, but God is also just. And there are times when He will use tough love on us all. I'm sure if my mother and daddy knew what I had done to Norma Jean, they would've taught me a lesson that would have caused extreme pain to my backside. But God wanted me to learn a lesson that would be lasting and change my heart.

I learned two things from my hair cut/Norma Jean experience:

1. Do unto others as you would have them do unto you.
2. First grade bangs can be humiliating at any age.

Verse of the Day:

Luke 6:31 "Do unto others as you would have them do unto you."

Reflections...

Can you recall a lesson in life taught by God instead of your parents?

Pray that God will do what only He can do in the life of your child or spouse. Name the area of their life that you feel is in need of change.

Thank Him that He has your family members in His hand.

Oh, Those Family Stories!

I included a chapter about my dad as a child. This story is about my mother. My mother was also a music teacher for a kindergarten program years ago. So, in essence, this is a Room 107 story, too. The following music room story is told in my mother's own words.

The Left Handed Pencil

"I taught music at a Methodist kindergarten, and when one of the teachers was out, I would substitute teach for them. I told the class to get their black crayon out, and a little boy, Jason, said, "Mrs. Henderson, I don't have a black one, I'll just use this red one."

I replied, "No, I will loan you a black crayon." Then I told them to get their pencil out, and print their names on the back of the paper.

I noticed little Jason looking at his pencil, and he said, "I can't use this pencil Mrs. Henderson, it doesn't have an eraser on it".

I said, "I will loan you an eraser." After I loaned him the eraser, he began twirling the pencil round and round in his tiny fingers.

Then he raised his hand yet again. I said, "Yes, Jason?"

He said, "Mrs. Henderson, I can't use this pencil because it is for a left handed person, and I am right handed."

-Charlotte Henderson

I loved when my mom came home with stories about her music students. Now I have my own stories to tell. My mother always encouraged me to be a music teacher, so I have her to thank for arriving at Room 107.

The boy with the left-handed pencil is like many of us. God asks us to do something and we find an excuse as to why we can't. The Lord has been prompting me for years to write a book. I ran out of excuses and finally decided to write! We are pros at excuse making!

I wonder if Noah made an excuse for building the ark? Or maybe he was just sold out to God so much that he started collecting wood at God's very first word to him.

And I think of Abraham. It seemed like he obeyed God right away when it came to sacrificing his son, Isaac. I wonder if he ever said, "I can't do that, God. This knife is for left handed people and I'm right handed." That's an extreme example, but you can probably get the picture. Abraham obeyed.

But when it came to Isaac actually being born, I think I relate more to Sarah than Abraham. Sarah was honest. Sarah doubted and Sarah laughed.

"Are you serious, God? Me, an old woman, bearing a child?" I can relate to that.

If Sarah lived today and texted, she would probably insert a big, "LOL" after telling her family that God was still saying she would have a son. I can just see her Facebook status: "So, how I am feeling today? Amused! God said I would have a baby! So what if I'm ninety something? LOL" Her hashtags might say, "#too-old-to-chase-toddlers #Abraham-is-no-spring-chicken."

At least she was honest. I am much like Sarah at times. Maybe you are, too.

We can be so religious that we give Sarah a hard time about laughing. But think about her reaction a minute. Do you know someone who is in their nineties? My grandmother is ninety-four years old. She has a lot of energy for someone her age, but it still takes her a few tries to get out of a chair. Can you imagine Sarah getting up all through the night with a crying child? No sleep at ninety something is tough for my grandmother, and I'm sure it was for Sarah. I would chime right in with Sarah's excuse not to receive God's promise. "God, I'm too old!" How many times have you told God that? It's your left-handed pencil for a right-handed dream.

There are promises that God has given me and I have waited years to receive. You probably have, too. I have had honesty moments with the Lord that have gone something like this:

"Lord, please don't wait and give me your promises when I'm ninety something like Sarah. I want to be young enough to enjoy them! And please don't make me wait too much longer."

Have you ever felt that way? But then I reconsider. What if God allowed Sarah to have a son late in life because He knew that at her age, it *would be* hard to raise and child? And what if He used that alone for His glory? What if the energy of a twenty year old suddenly kicked in after Isaac was born? And what if everyone was amazed at Sarah taking care of this baby because God helped her?

That's what God does. When He tells us to "take our crayons or pencils of life" and draw a picture of the promise that He's given us, He provides what we need. He provides the energy. He provides the resources. He provides, period. And He does it in a way that He alone will get the glory.

And just like Abraham, when He asks us to draw a picture of faithfulness for others to see, He provides every color of grace needed for that picture. Even if you feel you have a left-handed pencil for a right-handed dream, believe in the promise He's given you. His word never fails.

Trust Him with your promise.

Verse of the Day:

Romans 4:3

"For the Scriptures tell us, "Abraham believed God, and God counted him as righteous because of his faith."

Reflections...

What is God asking you to believe about Him today? What promise has He made that you have yet to see? Take a step of faith and offer Him your words of faith to receive it.

"An excuse is a skin of a reason stuffed with a lie."

~Billy Sunday

Prayer in School

Anyone who teaches school knows that prayer is nowhere near being shoved out the doors of public education. As the saying goes, "As long as there are tests, there will be prayers." It's true. Teachers pray. Students pray. Parents pray. We all pray. And during the "moment of silence" held each morning, you better believe we are probably all praying for a peaceful day.

I remember a day in Room 107 when my CD player stopped working, and we had no way to play our music. The kids were so disappointed. I tried plugging it in one last time to see if it would work, but no luck.

One little boy shouted out, "Your CD player needs prayer, Ms. Thrower!" I agreed. It surely needed prayer. I think it simply needed to be trashed.

Then another student shouted, "Hey, Hunter, get up and pray for that CD player!" Everyone started clapping for Hunter.

Another student blurted out, "Ms. Thrower, you should hear Hunter pray. He can get your CD player to work again! He prays like a preacher, Ms. Thrower!" One by one they all started giving Hunter high fives, slapping him on the back, urging him to step up to the CD player and pray.

Hunter, who was normally a quiet little boy in class, gladly accepted the challenge. He walked up to our CD player, looked at me, and said, "May I, Ms. Thrower?"

I said, "You sure can!"

Hunter paused for a second and silence fell on room 107. Hunter then took a deep breath and we sat in amazement as he let out what I call a Holy Ghost-Power House Prayer. When he finally said, "Amen," the class roared in applause. My CD player began to play and we enjoyed music that we had not heard in weeks! God hears all of our prayers, big or small!

Then there was the time with a praying parent…

I had broken my foot one year at school. One of our chorus parents let me use his relative's Jazzy battery operated wheel chair to maneuver around school. I was on break in my room when another chorus parent dropped by to see me. He asked how I was doing. I told him that I had just returned from the doctor's office with a report that the foot had not healed at all. It would probably take a few more months and I was discouraged.

The parent began telling me how God had touched his legs when he was a little boy. He was crippled and wore leg braces. His mother attended a Pentecostal church service and took him to the altar for prayer. His legs were healed and he threw away the braces! He wasn't even supposed to be walking at all, according to his doctors.

After listening to his story, I told him, "Well, if God can do that for you, He can do the same for me and heal my foot. Would you mind saying a prayer for me when you think about it?"

He told me he would pray. I was thinking that maybe he would go home and pray, or maybe he would even forget, but that was not the case.

He said, "Let's pray right now, Ms. Thrower.

The first thing that came to my mind was, "Is he going to do like Hunter, and pray a really loud, Holy Ghost filled prayer, and get me trouble at this school? What if it disrupts everyone's class? And what if someone walks by who doesn't understand? And what if, and what if, and what if?" I decided to let fear go, and trust him to pray. Besides, my foot hurt so badly, I was ready for anyone to lay hands on it and pray.

He gently removed his cowboy hat, laid his hand on my foot, and quietly prayed, "Lord, please heal Ms. Thrower's foot." That was it. Just six little words, and it was done.

He stood to his feet, put his hat back on and said, "Ms. Thrower, you'll be able to run on that foot tonight." And with a tip of his hat, and a smile, he left.

After school, on my way home, I noticed that I was driving a little faster than normal, and decided to slow down. I was not able go above the speed limit at all that morning when driving to school. In fact, I barely kept the speed limit in the weeks prior to that because it hurt to bare down on the accelerator. I thought to myself, "Could this be an answer to his prayer? The doctor said my foot was not healing at all yet."

When I arrived home, I got out of my car and stepped on the ground. I had no pain whatsoever! My boot was in the car, and I always had to put it on to walk. I wanted to see if I could walk without it and I could. I went inside my house. There is a long stretch from my kitchen to the master bedroom.

I remembered the gentleman telling me, "You'll be able to run on that foot when you get home, Ms. Thrower."

Dare I? What if I fall and break my leg?

I could just see me explaining this one to the doctor, "I know you said my foot wasn't healed, but this man prayed over me, and ..." I could just see my doctor shaking his head at me. But I decided to believe the words spoken in the simple prayer. I could run, I could hop, I could jump, and I bet if I knew how, I could have done a back flip, too!

I called my mom and dad to tell them the good news. I also invited them to come to my house to prove that I could run. They came, of course, but when they arrived, I was flat on my back, unable to move at all from the pain of my foot.

I explained to my parents, "I was just really wanting to believe that God healed my foot. I should've known better. I think I've broken it further now."

My mom took me back to the doctor the next day for more x-rays. I felt like such a fool. I should've known I couldn't run on a broken foot. At any rate, when the doctor returned to my room carrying two x-rays, he placed them on the lighted board for mom and me to see.

He said, "Ms. Thrower, do you see the crack in the first x-ray from earlier this week?"

I did. I saw it. I prepared myself for a sermon on how I needed to be patient and heal. I just knew the next x-ray would show my foot broken in two.

Then he pointed out the new x-ray and said, "Do you see this x-ray? It's completely smooth now, Ms. Thrower."

It was completely smooth. No break at all.

My doctor continued, "Your foot is healed, Ms. Thrower. I don't know how it healed so fast when you were just in here a few days ago and it showed no sign of improvement, but as you can see, it's smooth."

"There must be some mistake," I said. If it's not broken, why can't I walk, and why am I still in such pain?"

My doctor said, "It's pretty simple, Ms. Thrower. You have tendinitis from running on it so much last night. With a little ice and Tylenol, you should be fine."

I couldn't wait to get home and call the man who had prayed for me. When I called him, he was so humble about it. He said, "Ms. Thrower, God is the One who healed you. I can't take any credit for His work. All I did was pray. I'm glad your foot is ok."

I learned much from that experience. Sometimes we think we have to pour out a thirty minute long prayer for God to hear us. That is simply not true. He touched my foot with a one liner prayer, "God, please touch Ms. Thrower's foot."

God only desires honest communication from us.

What about you? How long has it been since you've prayed? If it's been a while, did you stop praying because you felt your words would fall to the ground? You're not alone if you've felt that way. Some of my most heartfelt, sincere prayers are the ones where I just yell out, "Help!!!"

God hears us. And He answers.

Verse of the Day:

James 5:16

"¹⁶ Confess your faults one to another, and pray one for another, that ye may be healed. The effectual fervent prayer of a righteous man availeth much."

Reflections...

When is the last time you talked to God?

What is broken in your life or body that you would like for Him to mend?

In a short sentence or a paragraph, ask Him to touch you.

Now thank Him that He heard your prayer. Thank Him for your brokenness.

Quiet Ones

In my career of teaching music, I've known two students who did not speak at school, but finally spoke or sang in music class. This story is about a little fifth grade girl. I'll call her, "Hannah."

I communicated with Hannah by giving her a high five when I passed her in the hall at school. She was very tall, and even though she didn't talk, I would always go up to her and say, "You know, we tall girls have to stick together." She would smile and give me a high five. But she never spoke a word.

However, there was this one time in Room 107.

My lesson plan for that day included playing a few pieces of instrumental music, and letting the children draw on paper what it sounded like to them. Anyone who is familiar with the musical pieces, "Flight of the Bumble Bee," "Carnival of the Animals," or "Syncopated Clock," knows that the music sounds much like the title. The violins in "Flight of the Bumble Bee" sound just like a real bumble bee. "The Syncopated Clock" sounds just like the real ticking of a clock. I decided to play these and a few others. It worked. As the children listened intently, most of them drew pictures that related to the title of the piece.

I decided to play, "Aquarium" from "Carnival of the Animals." If you listen closely to this piece, it gives the impression of running water. Some of my students think it sounds like "dreaming music." So, I played it, and the kids listened and drew their pictures.

When the piece was finished, I asked the class, "So, what did you draw?" From the back of the classroom, my little high fiving-silent friend shouted out, "Water!"

What I wanted to do next was jump up and down, run around the room, and do cartwheels down the hall of the school. But I decided to play it cool.

I acted as if she had always spoken and said, "You're right! It is water. It's called, "Aquarium. Good for you!"

She went back to drawing on her paper. I went back to teaching, but still had the urge to make a hallelujah run. She never said another word to me the rest of the year. As far as I know, she went right back into her quiet world for the rest of the year.

But my mind will always hear the music of her voice. That musical miracle moment of, "Water," will always be a song sung over and over in the back of my mind.

I think about that little girl and I think about us all. If God can move on her lips to speak, "Water," He can also move on our hearts to recognize His rushing flow. My prayer is that one day she will know the true Living Water.

Maybe one day she will say His Name, Jesus.

Verse of the Day:

John 4:14

"…but whoever drinks the water that I give them will never thirst. Indeed, the water I give them will become in them a spring of water welling up to eternal life."

Reflections...

When our spirits become thirsty, we can reach for the world to quench our thirst, or reach for God. How have you been reaching for the world to satisfy your thirst?

Pray and open God's word to read. What verses did He show you that quenched your thirst or watered a dry place in your life?

John 4:13 "¹³ Jesus answered, "Everyone who drinks this water will be thirsty again, ¹⁴ but whoever drinks the water I give them will never thirst. Indeed, the water I give them will become in them a spring of water welling up to eternal life."

R n' R

Everyone needs a little R and R. I can't help but laugh when kindergarten arrives to music at 10:30 a.m., already exhausted from the day, and ready to go home to momma!

Sometimes I feel like that, don't you? I get tired and exhausted before the task of the day gets started. I'm tired just thinking about it. Unlike kindergarteners, we can't just lie down and quit our projects. But we sometimes lie down and quit in our prayer lives, don't we?

How many times have you prayed and fallen asleep during a sentence? I have, more times than I care to admit. Maybe if we realize that prayer is simply a conversation with God, it won't seem like such a task. It doesn't have to be a long prayer. We can talk to God when we're driving, cleaning house, or in the shower. We can talk to God anytime, anywhere. Someone once asked me, "What time of day do you pray?" My answer to him was, "All day!" I talk to God in spurts throughout the day. My friend talks to God on his knees at a scheduled time and that's ok, too. All that matters is that we keep talking to The Lord. God promises us that He will answer us. He may not answer in our timing. He may not even answer the way we think He should. All that matters is that we keep talking to Him and trust Him. He will answer. Don't give up!

Verse of the Day:

Galatians 6:9

"Let us not become weary in doing good, for at the proper time we will reap a harvest if we do not give up."

Reflections...

Have you grown tired of praying for something in your life? What is it?

Galatians 6:9 promises us we will reap a harvest if we don't _____ ____.

If you knew that just one more prayer would be key to God granting what you've been asking of Him, what would you pray? Write it below:

Sheri Learns to Tell Time

The following is an excerpt from an article I wrote that was featured in a gospel music e-publication. I will meet you at the end of the story for its application.

"I wear many hats in music, and one of those is being a public school music teacher. I could write a book on the funny things children say and do. I bet a few of our former teachers could have written a book, too.

My story begins in first grade. Come with me to Lakeview Elementary.

One morning after roll call, my teacher asked the class, "Does anyone in the class know how to tell time?"

Well, I, The Little Miss Teacher Pleaser, raised my hand.

"I do!" I shouted.

My teacher looked over her black-framed glasses at me, and said, "Sheri…are you sure?"

"Yes!" I blurted out confidently.

My teacher reluctantly sent me out of the room to find a huge round clock placed high on the brick wall outside our door. She asked me to report back, and tell her what number the hands were on. I skipped out into the hall, found the big round clock, stared at it for a minute, and then whispering the time over and over so I would not to forget it, returned to the classroom.

"It is seventy o'clock, ma'am!" I said.

"Seventy o'clock? What do you mean?" she answered.

I took my teacher by the hand to the big clock outside the door, and pointing to the long red hand on it, I said, "See? The big hand is on the seventy. Seventy o'clock, ma'am!"

My teacher smiled, patted me on the head, and said, "Yes, honey, the hand *is* on the seventy. *That* is the temperature. Let me show you the *clock*."

I, along with my whole first grade class, learned that day that I didn't know a New York minute about telling time. Hopefully, I learned a greater lesson; I don't know as much as I think I do about a lot of things. I need someone to show me a thing or two. It's important to be teachable.

It's not easy being teachable. We like to figure things out for ourselves. We have the attitude of "I've got this." You name it, we know about it, and are ready to teach the class on it. We've been there, done that, and have the t-shirt.

Most of us don't even like following manuals. And we wonder why our newly assembled bicycles and swing sets look like mangled tinker toys on Christmas Eve.

Scripture talks about seeking instruction and looking for the manual in our lives. Sometimes the manual is found in other people.

Proverbs 15:22 states, "Plans fail for lack of counsel, but with many advisers, they succeed."

2 Timothy 2:15 says, "Study to show yourself approved unto God, a workman that needs not to be ashamed, rightly dividing the word of truth."

Seek advice. Study the manual.

It helps to get help. I remember sending the first few songs I had ever written to a publishing company in Nashville. I never read "the manual" on songwriting. I didn't know there was one, but I quickly found that after a two- page critique, kindly telling me that my songs needed improvement, (Insert a big "Ouch" here for critiques) I felt like that little first grader, wondering how to tell time. Just as my first grade teacher pointed me to the real clock, some helpful publishers pointed me to some great books and music schools to learn about song writing. I attended The Steve Hurst School of Music, where I now teach songwriting, and voice. I'm thankful for their influence. I "read their manual" and it changed my world."

This article points out the importance of learning from others. Be teachable. I have been blessed with songs on the charts in gospel music today because I sat at the feet of someone smarter than I who taught me to write. I have won awards in choral music and video production only because I was willing to ask for help at the feet of someone. I learned from those people.

I also had to trust God's timing to orchestrate those events in my life.

Five-year-old Sheri Henderson thought she knew how to tell time, but she had to learn to tell time from someone smarter than she. Can I be honest? I'm still learning to tell time. I'm still learning that life is all about God's timing.

The timing of writing this book has been of utmost importance. I've always wanted to write books. I thought my book would be about being a single mom and trusting God for provision. God showed me the clock in the hallway of His will and told me that "Miracles in Room 107" was the avenue He wanted me to take.

I am writing this book, thanks to the instruction of my S.W.A.T. writing class and writing instructor, Laura Brown. This class helped me realize that God has had a purpose for me teaching all of these years, when I preferred to be on the road singing. He had a reason for me being discouraged back in the college basement classrooms of 101-106, so that His timing would be perfect and lead me to room 107 with stories of His faithfulness. Only God could orchestrate even the numbers of those classrooms.

Only God could orchestrate the S.W.A.T writing class roster so that there would be an opening for one more person, me. And The Lord knows that I speak at Ann Downing's Middle Tennessee Women's Retreat each year during the last week of April. He knows I have always wanted to take along a book sharing my story. Well, it just so happens that this book, <u>Miracles in Room 107,</u> is due to be published the last week of April. God's timing is incredible. It is impeccable.

I'm learning to trust God's timing. Will you join me? Through the stories of this book, will you look beyond the words, and see the true miracles of Room 107? As my daughter told me, "Mom, you *are* Room 107." God has done a great miracle work in my life.

The timing of your entrance into room 107 is not by accident. God has you in the stories of this room for a purpose. His timing is perfect. Could it be that you are reading this book because now is the time to hear what God is and has been trying to say to you for years? Maybe you've just started listening today.

Could it be that the clock is striking midnight in your life? You need a twelve o' one experience. You need midnight to turn to day. This book is the chiming of that hour for you.

The Lord has led you to room 107 for a reason. Ask Him to reveal that to you now.

It's time.

Verse of the Day:

Psalm 31:15

"My times are in your hands; deliver me from the hands of my enemies, from those who pursue me." NIV

Reflections...

How has God's timing been better than yours lately?

What events has God perfectly orchestrated to place you where you are today?

How has reading this book been God's perfect timing in your life?

Sheri H. Thrower

"My times are in your hands; deliver me from the hands of my enemies, from those who pursue me."

Psalm 31:15

The Intruder

This story took place at a school where I once taught. Any teacher who has taught in a trailer behind the school can relate.

The intercom was broken in this little room, which was actually a trailer that sat to the side of the school. My phone wasn't working, and the door on the trailer would get stuck at times, too. It was not the most ideal situation should an emergency happen, but this school was in a great community, and the likelihood of anything life threatening happening was small.

Or so it seemed…

A class of second graders showed up for music. Most days, their teacher would wait at the corner of the school building and watch them as they entered the trailer. However, on this day, she must have left before the last child closed the door.

All of the children came in and took their usual seats on the floor. Music class began.

During the middle of a song I was teaching, in walked in a tall, unkempt stranger who looked to be in his early twenties. My heart sank because he did not have on a visitor's sticker. In fact, he didn't even knock. He just walked in. He slowly circled around my classroom, looking at each child. He stopped in the middle of the room and looked at me.

"May I help you?" I asked.

"No, I'm just watching," he said.

He was acting very strange.

All I could think was, "I am going to die in this trailer, right here, right now, along with all these precious children."

I did not have a cell phone with me to call for help either.

I thought, "Well, if I'm going to die, I might as well die singing."

So I asked him, "Do you like to sing?"

He said, "As a matter of fact, I love to sing!"

Wiping the sweat from my brow, I said, "Well, let's sing! Boys and girls, our new friend is going to sing with us!"

Then I said, "I'll tell you what…we'll sing you a song, then you can sing it with us. Sound good?"

He said, "Sounds good."

I thought, "Oh. My. Goodness. If I can just keep him singing until their teacher shows up to go get me some help!"

So, I played every kid's song I ever knew on the piano. I played "Jingles Bells," and it wasn't even Christmas. Even still, he sang along.

I was running out of songs, so I said, "Hey, do you like hymns?"

I thought to myself, "If I'm going to die, at least I'll try winning him to the Lord, first, with a good hymn that has great theology for salvation."

He looked at me puzzled. Then he made his way closer to the piano.

I thought to myself, "This is it! He's going to shoot me in the back of the head in front of all these babies."

My heart pounded out of my chest. So, I started playing and singing, "Amazing Grace." I sang that song from my toes! The more I sang it, the faster it got. I've never felt the meaning of those lyrics any more than at that moment when my life was about to end.

With my voice shaking, I asked him, "D-D-Do you know this h-h-hymn? I love this h-h-hymn."

He said, "Yes, I've heard it, but I don't know all the words."

I said, "That's ok. I'll sing it again. We'll *all* sing it again! And *you* can join in."

I sang every verse of that song, and probably made up a few verses with it, just hoping and praying someone would open that music room door to save the day.

Finally, the class's teacher arrived. I could finally breathe. She walked in my room, smiled at me, and started lining the kids up to leave. I was trying to act nonchalant, but how does one act nonchalant when they know they're probably going to be murdered within the next sixty seconds after the door closes? I excused myself from the piano and from our "new friend," and went over to the teacher, darting my eyes back to the man still at the piano. I was trying to give her a hint that I was in trouble, but it wasn't working. She probably thought I had a nervous twitch. She looked at me as if to say, "Are you ok today?"

She did not get my hint.

Our new visitor started making his way towards the other teacher and myself.

He looked at me, smiled, and said, "Excuse me. I've had a good time. Thank you."

Then he left. Was that it? Where was he going next? I had to save the rest of the school! I watched him walk into the brick school building. I ran all the way to the front office to warn my principal and call 911.

I found my principal waiting in his office. I talked a million miles a minute, with tears in my eyes telling him about the intruder in the trailer, and how he needed to call 911. I told him how I distracted him from killing us all by singing hymns and playing, "Jingle Bells." And I felt terrible that the intruder got away, but I was sure he was somewhere in the building.

My principal laughed and informed me that the intruder was a friend of his. His friend had a day off and wanted to spend it with him. He had asked him what would be a good class would be for him to visit, so the principal said, "the music room!"

I went home and crashed from the drama of my would-be-killer-intruder. I was so thankful it was not what it seemed. On occasions like that, you hold your kids a little tighter at night. I held mine tighter. We laughed talking about how I sang with the intruder.

Later, that year, the school had a lock down because a runaway fugitive was in our area. He was seen on our playground, and was hiding in the woods next to the school. Our principal cornered him and called the police.

Me? I had all I could take of intruders for the week.

I was fresh out of hymns and humor. However, humor has been and always will be in my survival kit.

Verse of the Day:

Psalm 32:7 "You are my hiding place; you will protect me from trouble and surround me with songs of deliverance." NIV

Reflections...

The stranger in this story was not an actual intruder. However, as Christians, we are very aware of the real intruder in our lives. He is the enemy of our souls.

The Word says in John 10:10 "[10] The thief comes only to steal and kill and destroy; I have come that they may have life, and have it to the full." The enemy may intrude in our families, our work place, or even in our thought life. In what area of your life is The Intruder trying to harass you?

God's word says that we overcome the enemy by the blood of The Lamb, and the word of our testimony.

Revelation 12:11 "They triumphed over him by the blood of the Lamb and by the word of their testimony; they did not love their lives so much as to shrink from death."

What is your testimony of God's grace? Write it. Read it out loud as your testimony against the enemy and his intrusions in your life. Jesus said He has come that you might have life and have it to the full. Thank Him for that right now, as you pray.

U Ain't S'posed to Cuss in School!

I never had the little boy in music class, but he always stopped by the music room on his way to lunch.

On several days he would wave at me through the window of my door. He would stick his head in my door yelling, "Hey! I wanna have lunch with you sometime!"

I said, "Ok, we will!" I never really took him seriously.

However, as I made my way through the lunch line one day, there he was.

My special needs little friend looked at me and said, "When are we going to have lunch together?"

I replied, "We will, we will. But I can't today. I'm sorry."

"No! I want to have lunch NOW! You can't put me off anymore, teacher."

What choice did I have? I invited this little guy to my room for lunch.

I had no idea who this little boy was, what grade he was in, or why he even wanted to eat lunch with me. I just knew it was important to him for some reason.

We arrived in room 107 with our lunch trays, and pulling out a chair, I said, "Here, have a seat." I asked him his name. He told me. Trying to start some kind of conversation, I asked him if he had brothers and sisters. That opened a can of worms. He began telling me his whole life story, and how hard life was for him. He shared how he could beat up anyone in his neighborhood. His dad told him that if somebody started something with him, he had better finish it. I heard story after story about beating up kids in his neighborhood, and making his daddy proud. I decided to just listen and let him talk. His story broke my heart. He had so much pinned up anger.

Then has asked me, "So, teacher. Are you married?"

The question caught me by surprise. However, considering this little boy seemed like a twenty year old in a ten-year-old body, it should not have surprised me. He was way ahead of his years in street smarts.

So, I answered him, "No, I am not married."

"Divorced?" he asked. Then he continued, "Was he a blankety blank, blank to ya?" (I will not repeat his actual words. Trust me. His words were vile.) After spewing that comment, he quickly put his hand over his mouth, and said, "Oh sorry! I'm supposed to be trying not to cuss at school! I keep forgetting! I'll do better. No more cussin! My dad cusses and it's hard to hear it from him and come to school and not do it."

I completely understood this little guy. We all emulate our parents. I had to make the decision to discipline this little guy for his inappropriate language, or try and understand him. So, I did both. I gently told him, "True. We can't use language like that at school. You can do it! Just keep reminding yourself. It's ok, buddy."

He looked at me and said, "Yeh…ya ain't s'posed to cuss at school."

It was almost time for my little friend to go, but as he got up from his lunch, he made his way around my room looking at all of the instruments.

He stopped and said, "Hey, you gotta guitar?" To which I replied,

"No, I'm sorry. No guitar."

He saw a drum and said, "That's ok. I can play it on this here drum. I have a song to sing ya!" I said, "Ok," and watched him make his way to a small drum in my room.

He picked up a drum stick, struck the drum two times, and said, "Nope. I can't play in this key. You gotta piano? I'll try to play it!"

I said, "I'll tell you what. Let me play the piano. You sing." Then I asked him, "Do you know the song, "Amazing Grace?" He said, "Nah, I don't think I know that one. Can you sing it?" I told him I would sing it for him.

I sang that old hymn for this little guy that I didn't know from Adam. He listened. He seemed to like the hymn, and would catch a few words here and there to sing with me.

It was time for him to go. His teacher came to the door to pick him up, and looked at me as if to say, "Was he ok?" I told her he was perfect.

That was the first and last time I ate with my little friend. As far as I know, he moved, and I never saw him again.

I learned a lot that day from that little guy. First of all, I learned that God orchestrated this lunch. He knew my little friend needed to talk. He knew I would play "Amazing Grace," for him. Someday, somewhere down the road, I hope this little boy remembers someone listening to his story, and not condemning his inherited vulgar language. Maybe someday he will think back to Room 107, and remember hearing a song about God's forgiving grace.

I am much like that little boy. Can you relate? We say and do things that need forgiveness. Our words are shocking. Whether we "cuss," or say sharp things, our words hurt. We are on the playground of life, beating everyone up around us with our words, only because we have been hurt, too. We need the school of holiness to enter our lives and apply needed discipline. And we need someone to balance it with a song of grace.

As my grandmother always says, "Cussin' is a lack-a-vocabulary." Maybe that's what I understood about this little "cussing friend" in room 107. He lacked vocabulary and love. He needed to be understood. He needed grace.

We all do.

Verse of the Day:

2 Corinthians 1:4

3"Blessed be the God and Father of our Lord Jesus Christ, the Father of mercies and God of all comfort, 4who comforts us in all our affliction so that we will be able to comfort those who are in any affliction with the comfort with which we ourselves are comforted by God."

Reflections...

Who in your life needs grace extended to them and why?

Who in your life has extended grace to you when you needed it?

How does our Verse of the Day speak to you?

@$#%!

"Cussin' is a lack-a-vocabulary"

-Sheri's grandmother

Very Zoe

Whenever I see or hear of something very compassionate or sweet, I will say, "That is very Zoe." Meet sweet little Zoe.

The first thing you'll notice about Zoe when she enters a room is the light in her eyes. She has the kindest eyes and the most positive attitude of most anyone I know. She's always smiling and always encouraging.

Zoe was born with a cleft palette and has had about twenty different cranial facial surgeries. Some children who are born with facial disfiguration are also known to have hearing problems. And people who have hearing problems sometimes have pitch problems and can't sing well. Not true of little Zoe. She can flat bring an audience quickly to their feet after she sings. Not only does she sing well, she has perfect pitch. Zoe rarely sings off pitch and if I had to guess, I would say she has a two octave range.

I gave her the solo, "Oh Holy Night" in our Christmas concert one year. I'll never forget the moment she sang the part of the song, "Oh night divine." I think she held the note on "divine" for three days and four hours. Well, it seemed like it! If you look at the YouTube video of her performance, you'll see her taking a huge breath, leaning way back and holding that note forever. You'll also see me approaching her, making sure she doesn't pass out while holding the note. More than this, you'll see the audience jumping to their feet with excitement at this little angel's voice. She's a little powerhouse.

After the Christmas concert that night, I had the privilege of meeting her grandparents. They said, "We had no idea that Zoe could sing, Ms. Thrower! This is a surprise to us all!"

I remember looking stunned at Zoe's family then saying, "You mean to tell me that Zoe doesn't sing in the shower, or around the house? You've really never heard her sing a solo until tonight?" The whole family agreed together that little Zoe had never shown them her voice until the night of our concert. With tears in their eyes, they explained how she had been telling them that she had been given a solo, but wanted to surprise them. And surprise them she did!

Zoe is one of those special people in the world. She's almost angelic-like. I've never known anyone to be sweet "twenty-four-seven," but Zoe is. Just ask her grandmother.

I spoke with her grandmother this morning, talking about Zoe's story and including it in my book. She told me something fascinating that I never knew until today. She shared with me how she had an afflicted baby some years back, but sadly, it died. Her world fell apart. But then her son and his wife had two little girls, and one of them was just like her baby that died. It was Zoe. She shared how she was happy to have a new grandbaby, but also cried because she knew the hard road that would be ahead for her son. He would have to endure people possibly making fun of his daughter and people looking at her, wondering what happened to her little face.

Then she began sharing with me the silver lining around the story. She told me how Zoe had changed her life. She said, "I believe Zoe is sent from heaven as an angel. I know the Lord used her to draw me back to Him, because I had even stopped going to church. Because of Zoe, I turned back to the Lord." She mentioned a time that Zoe spoke about angels when she said, "La La, do you know we have angels?" This sweet grandmother told about how Zoe referred to her as a personal angel in her little life. Zoe's grandmother told Zoe that she believed Zoe was her angel, as well.

Zoe's family thanks me quite often for my work with her as her teacher. But I'm the one who should thank them. When I've missed school this year, Zoe sends me Facebook messages saying, "I'm praying for you!" It's not uncommon throughout my day at school that the door will open, and little Zoe pops in just to give me a hug and smile, then goes on her merry way. I had to go home early one day from getting sick in class and Zoe sent me one of her uplifting messages on Facebook, asking me how I was. And once again, she said she was praying for me. She sends little chain letters, as well, saying, "If you pass this to ten people, God will answer two of your biggest needs today!" Yes, she's a little angel to me, too. I agree with her grandmother on that.

I don't notice Zoe's affliction. I notice her heart. I notice her compassion and her genuine concern. I simply notice her little spirit. And I love it. And I wish I were more like her.

I look at Zoe and others I've known like her, and notice something different. People who suffer, or have suffered much, share something that many of us don't seem to have. I call it an aroma. It's a fragrance. And it's a sweet fragrance. It is Christ with skin and bones. Jesus suffered. And when we suffer, or have been broken, we are more Christ-like than any other time in our lives.

As much as I desire to be compassionate like Zoe, I know I may never be quite like her. I've never suffered like her.

We all suffer in one way or another. Some have suffered their marriages breaking up. Some have suffered the death of a child. Some may have suffered minimally. The question to ask is, "What have we done with our suffering? Have we become more compassionate to others, or have we become more self-righteous because we "made it through?" Have we become humble by our suffering? Or have we become arrogant because we gained a victory or healing?

King David, in the book of Psalm, said something I find both beautiful and interesting when he said this in Psalm 119: 71:

"It was good for me to be afflicted so that I might learn your decrees."

David learned God's decrees because he was afflicted. That's the blessing of affliction. Affliction is our teacher. Affliction is our humbler. And affliction is always our challenge as Christians. We have a choice to be humbled by our personal affliction, or become arrogant because we survived it. And when someone is humble, they never have to even mention the word. They simply demonstrate it.

No matter what challenges face little Zoe, her catch phrase is always, "I've got this!" If Zoe can say that while having challenges of breathing, hearing, and even enduring other hardships, I can say it, too.

I want to be very Zoe. Not only do I want to say, "I've got this" about life's challenges, I want to say that about being more loving and compassionate.

And looking at our life circumstances, maybe we should all be like David to say, "It was good for me to be afflicted."

Verse of the Day:

Psalm 119:71

"It was good for me to be afflicted so that I might learn your decrees."

Reflections:

Describe a time in your life where you have suffered? (On your job, in your health, in your marriage, etc.)

What fruit of the spirit did it produce in your life?

Pray and ask God to move you with compassion for the lost.

When a Student Dies

My little sister, Rhonda died when she was only two years old. I was three. I remember her well. She was my buddy and my best friend. And I miss her even now.

I remember the day she died. My mom told me that the angels came to get her. I remember staring straight ahead, and my three-year- old mind thinking about that vision. I was ok with that picture. After all, heaven and angels are soothing thoughts for children to think about.

As I am writing this book, I found out that one of my former chorus members just died in a tragic car accident. This is the third or fourth student that has passed away during my teaching career.

My little chorus member was only sixteen when she got killed this week. Her little niece is in one of my kindergarten music classes. She came to music today.

Her usual demeanor is upbeat and energetic. Today, she quietly walked to my desk and snuggled close to my side. I knew why. I just looked into her eyes, waiting for her to say what I knew she would say.

Then she spoke, "Ms. Thrower, my aunt went to be with Jesus the other day."

As I looked into the sad eyes of this distraught child, I could see her aunt's eyes staring back at me. She looked so much like her.

So, I did what every teacher does in those moments. I dug back into this experience of my life and I responded with, "I know, sweetie. And guess what? She is up in heaven with my sister!"

"You have a sister in heaven, Ms. Thrower?" she said excitedly.

"Yes, I do!" I said.

What's her name?" she asked.

I said, "Rhonda."

"Rhonda?" she asked.

"Yes, and I bet you anything they are up there playing together. Don't you think? I bet the very day your aunt went to heaven, my little sister ran up to her and said, "Hey! Do you know my sister, Sheri Thrower? Weren't you in her chorus?" I bet they are playing "London Bridges" together and "Ring Around the Roses," too. Whatcha bet?"

This sad little angel's eyes became bright with hope as she said, "Yeh! I bet she is playing with your sister! Wow!"

I said, "They are having so much fun! Heaven is a wonderful place."

She agreed, smiled and sat down.

I think every Christian teacher will agree; we don't have to say a word during times like these. Although I tried comforting this little girl with a story about heaven, we don't have to say a word. Our hugs say so much. Our pats on the back say it, too. The light of Christ can never be dimmed, for it shines in all the mentioned above; our hugs, our understanding eyes, our pats on the back…in our love.

And perhaps, the greatest miracle will be people understanding this.

Verse of the Day:

2 Corinthians 1:3-4: "Blessed be the God and Father of our Lord Jesus Christ, the Father of mercies and God of all comfort, who comforts us in all our affliction, so that we may be able to comfort those who are in any affliction with the comfort with which we ourselves are comforted by God."

Reflections...

Describe a time in your life when you needed comfort the most.

How can you use your story to help someone else?

Sheri H. Thrower

"We are all a little broken,
But last I checked, even broken crayons
Still color the same." -unknown

X Husbands Come to Music

Word travels fast in a small town. When I first became single again, word got out and several of my boy students wanted to set "Ms. Thrower" up with their single dads. Even though this did not happen in Room 107, it is part of my teaching years in education. Again, I like to think that everywhere I go is a "107" experience.

Two little boys told me that their dads were joining them in music class that week. It happened. Their dads came to music class. Should I have been flattered? I think flattered and awkward need to combine and create a word as to how I felt. The word would be, "Flatkward."

The first single dad showed up in a cowboy hat, boots, tight Wrangler jeans, and a big smile. He also donned a tan leather, opened front vest with long fringe hanging from each side. The "Waffle House" logo was embedded on the back, and he was not wearing a shirt. Can we say, "Flatkward?"

A woman knows how to give the "I'm not interested" signal. I didn't want to hurt my little student's feelings, nor his fathers, but I did want try and seem less attractive to our new visitor. So, I did what any good music teacher would do, I invited him to get up and move with us. Hokey Pokey Style!

By the time we were finished huffing and puffing through The Hokey Pokey, I think every vision and dream of being this little boy's next momma was "Hokey Pokied" right out of the room.

But there was the time when another dad came to music and did actually ask me out after class. He was about three feet shorter than me. I think the awkwardness of looking up at my 5"7 stature when asking me out, was enough to quickly change his mind.

While there is a light, humorous side to "X Husbands Come to Music Class," there is a serious side that cannot be ignored. And it saddens me. Children want a family. These little boys did. All children do. They want family, and they want their families mended. They missed their mothers. And in their minds, finding a replacement was a priority. I'm sure they just wanted to see their dads happy again. They probably wanted some healthier meals, too. Little did they know that Ms. Thrower is not a gourmet cook. I should've brought my cooking for their dads to eat, instead of having them do The Hokey Pokey.

Broken homes are the norm today. I know because I have one. I have seen my children, who are now grown and in college, go through life raised in the heartache of divorce, and it's heart breaking to watch.

No wonder divorce is mentioned in the Bible as one of the things God hates. I think everyone who has experienced the shame of divorce will agree with God. We hate it, too.

And just like the dads who came to music class with hopes that they could possibly find a mom for their sons, we all have been known to get desperate looking for a fix to our family dysfunction. We participate in "The Hokey Pokey's of life, "doing all the moves required, trying to find some sort of answer. We dance with drugs, alcohol, relationship, after relationship, trying to fill the void. We put our best face in, we take our best face out. We put our morals in, we take our morals out, and we think "being happy" is what it's all about. We forget that being holy is really what it's all about.

We totally dance around scripture, ignoring the principles and peace of mind that are found there. We dance around God's voice, because the music of our self-will is so loud, we can't hear Him speak. We turn up the volume of our own selfish dance music, and drown out peace. And we huff and puff when the dance is over because we are worn out from searching for peace in the wrong places.

Maybe we just need to slow down, rest, and wait in faith.

We put our faith in, and we never take it out. That's what it's all about.

Verse of the Day:

Isaiah 40:31 "But they that wait upon the Lord shall renew their strength; they shall mount up with wings as eagles; they shall run, and not be weary; and they walk, and not faint."

Reflections...

What do you feel impatient about today?

What does God's word from Isaiah 40: 31 tell you to do?

Read the full chapter of Isaiah 40. What is The Holy Spirit saying to you through this passage today?

"I was addicted to the Hokey Pokey...but I turned myself around."

—Unknown

Yes, I Stutter. Yes, I Sing

Two of the biggest miracles I've seen is a stuttering child sing, and what some people may call, " selectively mute," speak and sing.

This story is about my little stutterer.

The first time I heard him talk, I couldn't believe my ears. He had a very difficult time communicating. He could barely speak one sentence without stumbling all over his words. My worst nightmare as a choral director was the day he auditioned for chorus.

I have to admit, I was a little nervous for him. I knew the struggle he went through just trying to talk. I could only imagine what his audition would be like. I was prepared to encourage him, although I assumed he probably would not make the cut. How could I explain to him that he wasn't quite ready to sing? Boy, was I wrong! This little boy could sing a full song without one flaw. Music flowed from his lips.

He made the audition for chorus, and to my surprise, auditioned for nearly every solo we had. I gave him several solos because he sang so well. He reminded me of country singer, Mel Tillis. Mel had a difficult time speaking due to his stuttering problem, but boy could he sing!

One day during chorus rehearsal, I noticed my little guy wasn't singing much. I just left him alone because I thought he may have had a bad day and needed some time to himself. However, when I dismissed the children to go home, he came up to me and wanted to talk. He just could not form his words that day at all. As hard as he tried, he could not communicate to me what was on his mind.

Finally, I said, "Hey, buddy…sing to me what you're wanting to say."

He looked at me so confused.

I said, "Sing it! Whatever you're trying to say, sing it!"

He paused for a minute, took a deep breath, and on his own made up tune, he sang, "I didn't sing in chorus today because I had a sore throat last night, and I took some medicine that made my throat real dry, and that's why I didn't siiiiiiiinnnnng todaaaaaay!"

To which I replied, "I hope you feel better, Bud!" I was thrilled that I found a new way to communicate with my little friend.

On the next rehearsal date, he tried out for a Christmas solo. He got the solo and when we performed the song at Christmas, he melted everyone's heart. We had a talent show later that year, and all of us found out that he could dance his feet off, as well. He brought the house down whenever he performed.

I watched this little boy go from not having many friends, to being loved by everyone. At the beginning of the year, everyone knew him as a stutterer. By the end of the year, everyone knew him as an incredible performer. And maybe that's the true miracle.

He chose not to be in chorus his last year at school. The reason was because he had made so many new friends that he wanted to be at our aftercare program at school. That was fine with me. I knew he needed friendships more than he needed chorus. I'm thankful how the Lord used music to open the door for peer acceptance in his life.

This student's story reminds me of the story of Moses in the Bible. Moses was a stutterer. When God asked him to go before Pharaoh saying, "Let my people go," Moses had a very normal reaction found in Exodus 4:10: "But Moses pleaded with the LORD, "O Lord, I'm just not a good speaker. I never have been, and I'm not now, even after you have spoken to me. I'm clumsy with words." NLT

Moses knew his limitations. He was a realist.

But God came to Moses, just as He comes to us in the middle of our real life limiting situations, and says what He said to Moses, "…who do you think made the human mouth?"(Exodus 4:11)

In other words, "Who made your mouth, Moses?"

I love that response from God. Moses had to trust and believe God's opinion of himself. That's another book to be written.

Maybe you, too, are limited by challenges. Just like Moses, and just like my little stutterer, God can use you in spite of your disabilities.

Even if we say, "Lord, you know I'm not smart enough. You know I can't talk. You know I'm divorced. You know I am a single mom. You know I've committed adultery."

How about this one? "Lord, You know I've sinned, and I can't stop."

Sin has a way of turning us into spiritual stutterers. Just when we're trying to speak our praise to God, or pray, we're reminded of our sin. That reminder stops us in our tracks, so we stop praying. We stop praising. We start to pray, and we stop. We start to praise, and we stop. We can't get the words out. We can't get our praise out. We stutter before God. That's what sin does to us. It separates us from fellowship with God, and with each other. It causes us to "stutter."

You've been there. I've been there, too. When we've blown it, we automatically place an "L" on our lives, meaning, "Loser: Can't be used by God." That is absolutely the biggest lie of the enemy, and he uses it each time we sin. The condemning voice in our conscience says we've crossed one line too many this time. It tells us that we are the only person in the world that struggles with sin. It condemns us to the point that we stutter. We sit back in the corner of our lives, become loners, and choose not to participate in what God has called us to do.

But God has a different idea for us. If you don't believe it, look at Moses. Look at Noah. And be sure to take a close look at King David. All three were men who failed miserably, but God used them anyway. Moses could've given up after a moment of anger, and smiting a rock, and stuttering. Noah could've called it quits with God after being found drunk and naked in a tent.

David could've said, "Forget it, God, You can't use an adulterous man."

God used them. God can use you.

You and I can do what God has called us to do when we give our weaknesses and inabilities to Him.

After all, it's really not about our ability. It's all about His.

Verse of the Day:

Philippians 4:13

"I can do all things through Christ which strengthens me." NKJV

Reflections...

How are you a spiritual stutterer? What is the besetting sin in your life that is keeping you from speaking your praise, or prayer to God?

Just as Moses was honest with God about His speech problem, we must identify and get real about our limitations. How do you feel useless to God and His church? Tell Him.

In your own words, tell The Lord that you are available to be used by Him, however He chooses. His power is perfected in your weakness

Zoom In On This

I have shared how Room 107 itself is a miracle. However, there is one final miracle about this room that I have saved for the last.

When I got married at twenty-six years old, I had a neatly wrapped packaged plan for my life. I, Cinderella of Perfection Land, would marry the flawless Prince Charming of Handsomeville. Together, we would serve God, and live happily ever after with our well-dressed, well-mannered, highly intelligent offspring. And we would shine for Jesus in our peaceful castle where I would never work. Ever. Again. Besides, this is God's way of parenting. Isn't it? A mother should stay at home with her children.

Now picture with me the scenes of Hiroshima. My peaceful castle on the hill was leveled to the ground like a sudden nuclear bomb attack. Unexpected strikes of difficulties destroyed every hope and dream for my family. Suddenly, I was a single mother, thrown back into the work force again. I had no teaching certificate, no job, and no bank account. I had my children, immediate family, and my faith. And my faith, hanging by a thread, led me to Room 107.

During the time of my marriage falling apart, the governor of our state made a ruling that if a teacher was not certified in the area they were teaching, they must step down immediately. A music teacher in our county where I used to teach was not certified, so she had to step down from her position. The school called me to see if I would like to take the job again and replace her. They even agreed to let me renew my certification while teaching because I did have a music degree. I accepted the position, and taught at that little school for three wonderful years.

However, one day, I passed the little school where my children attended. I used to teach there before my children were born. My daughter was in the fourth grade during this time. Driving past the school, I prayed, "Oh, God, if You could just give the music teacher at my daughter's school a job she can't refuse, I would love to teach there so that I can be with her during the day. I am thankful for my job at the little school where I teach now, but I really miss being with her. I have missed some years with her and my son. I just want to be with my child again."

The next week, the principal from my daughter's school called me and said, "Sheri, the music teacher at our school has received another job offer she can't refuse, and is leaving. Would you consider coming back?"

I jumped at the chance to go back. Since a classroom was not available, I had to push a music cart room to room for a few years, and even had my office in a storage closet, but it was worth it. I finally ended up in a "real classroom"; Room 107.

It's been a wonderful journey here. I look back and smile while also wiping my tears. Much has happened in this room. Photographs fill the walls and bulletin boards with memories the children and I have made together. In addition to being the classroom music teacher, I also direct our wonderful award-winning chorus. I see memories of where we performed at Radio City Music Hall in New York City. There are photos of us at Disney World, America's Got Talent Auditions, The Nation's Capitol Building and more. Four music trophies are displayed on our bookcase from where they won some competitions, as well.

We dreamed it. We achieved it. Together. God has blessed my years here.

I look at the beautiful memories made with these children, and yet I am haunted by something that was said to me while going through the heartache of my marriage break up. The church that I attended at the time of my divorce did not believe me when I told them that my marriage was failing. Before testifying against me in court one day for "fabricating the problems in my marriage," I was told, "Sheri, you know your ministry is over, right? You will never sing again due to this. Your music ministry will die. God will not bless this."

That statement was a dagger to my soul. At the same time I knew the call of God on my life, and His word in Romans 11: 29 says, "God's gifts and God's call are under full warranty-never canceled, never rescinded."*(The Message)*

I realized that although my fellow brothers in The Lord refused to look at the devastating effects of divorce in my home, my Heavenly Father looked at the situation with compassion, and eyes of provision and truth. I'd like to pause here and say sometimes people make assumptions based on their lack of knowledge about a situation. Let go of the grudge! God is truth, and He knows how to shed light on darkness. Don't let darkness live in your heart by resenting people who don't understand you or what you're going through.

Not only did the Lord provide Room 107 as a place of provision for my needs as a single mother, He made it a place of continued ministry. Anywhere our chorus sang, we included a gospel song in our set of secular music. For years, we have sung the spiritual, "Amen," from the movie, "Lilies of the Field." The song, in only four short minutes, tells of the birth, life, death, burial, and resurrection of Jesus. From north and south to east and west, our public school chorus has shared the gospel through this song and others. New York's, "BB King Jazz Club" has heard it. "Hard Rock Café" in D.C., has too. Audiences all over YouTube land have heard it as well. We've shared the gospel. That's quite a miracle for a public school chorus. Gospel music is a part of our American heritage, and teaching it is a part of our state standards. It may come as a surprise that it is included along with the many genres of music we are required to teach. Our chorus has sung most every genre.

Has including gospel music in our concerts made a difference? I have to believe it has, even if I don't see it. Have I seen lives saved from singing the gospel? Yes, I have. One of my students became a Christian later in life, marrying a minister of the gospel. She contributes her salvation partly due to hearing gospel music that our show choir sang in high school. I'm thankful to the Lord for her.

Although I'm thrilled to hear stories like this, I have to remind myself that it is not my job to see the results. That is God's job. My job is to plant a seed. I have planted a seed. I trust God for it to grow.

Just this past year, a former member of our chorus passed away. I'm thankful that she became a Christian while attending the "Good News Club". Good News is a national Christian organization that is offered after school to elementary school students. I'm thankful that she heard the gospel there and that she also sang its message through Christmas concerts with our choir. She's with Jesus now. I pray our music played a role in that. That's real ministry to me.

I've had to reevaluate my concept of ministry. For years, I looked at the exciting stages where I've performed as ministry. I've looked at women's retreats where I've spoken as the place of real ministry. While those places are very real platforms for ministry, I've come to realize that this classroom is a ministry, too. In fact, it's probably the most important ministry in my life other than my role as mother. And in light of this, I have come to a place of forgiveness in my heart to those who said ministry would end for me. In fact, I received an apology years later.

An apology is healing, isn't it? It makes forgiving easier. However, I know the Lord would require me to forgive if an apology were never given. And that's hard. Sometimes it's a daily challenge. But I am thankful for God's grace to forgive. I'm also thankful He placed my children and me in a new church family where we are accepted, loved, and can now serve. We had to move on, and it's ok to move on. We do have good memories from our former church. It wasn't all hurt and pain. I have come to learn that people make mistakes, and sometimes lack of knowledge will cause people to make wrong judgments. However, God is our vindicator and He makes everything right. Truth always stands. If I had known the truth that my situation was going to finally come to light, I would not have shed so many tears about it in the beginning. I would've trusted God more. We live and learn.

Through these hurtful experiences, I had to come to terms with why I serve Jesus. I continue in ministry because of Him. I serve His Body because of Him. He is my reason. He is my focus. If I lose sight of my focus, I lose my purpose. It's all about Him. People will let us down. Jesus never will. I have also learned that it's not who I am that is important, but Whose I am. I am a child of God.

As His child I know that forgiveness is not easy, but an unforgiving spirit can break our fellowship with God. Forgiveness is one of the ABC's of life I've learned from children. They forgive and they forget. No wonder Jesus tells us to become like a child to enter His kingdom. He wants us to follow their example in many ways; most importantly, to be real. Children are real.

I plan to leave room 107 at the end of this year. I feel my time is complete, as I enter the next phase of my life in music and ministry. I am thankful for these sweet children who have taught me great life lessons. While it is true that students learn from their teachers, I must say, I have learned more from them. I thank them for teaching me the following ABC's of life:

    A: Always hug

    B: Be real.

    C: Create something out of nothing

    D: Dance to the music in your heart

    E: Express yourself

    F: Forgive. Forgive. Forgive.

    H: Have friends

    I: Invite others to play

    J: Jesus Loves Me is the greatest theology

    K: Kick off your shoes and have fun

    L: Love unconditionally

M: Make mistakes and erase

N: Nap

O: Open your eyes to the beauty of simple things

P: Practice generosity

Q: Quitting is not an option

R: Rest, play, rest, play

S: Say, "I love you" often

T: Tell someone they look nice everyday

U: Unleash your inner rock star

V: View life in moments

W: Wait your turn

X: Exit the building quietly

Y: Yell when you're happy

Z: Zoom in on what God is doing in your pain and pleasure.

I pray that this book has encouraged your walk with Christ. I trust you will learn to see His miracles around you every day. I pray that you have heard God's voice and know that our final Verse of the Day, from Ephesians 3: 20, is true when it says:

"Now unto him that is able to do exceeding abundantly above all that we ask or think, according to the power that works in us, **21**to him be glory in the church and in Christ Jesus throughout all generations, for ever and ever! Amen."

God is able to do the "exceedingly above all" in your life. In other words, He is able to do a miracle. He can and will do a "Room 107" in and for you.

Believe.

Verse of the Day:

Ephesians 3:20

"Now unto him that is able to do exceeding abundantly above all that we ask or think, according to the power that works in us, **21**to him be glory in the church and in Christ Jesus throughout all generations, for ever and ever! Amen."

Reflections...

What miracle do you recognize in your life today?

What do you want or need God to do in your life that is exceedingly above all you could ask or think?

In the ABC list of what I've learned from children, which one do you relate to most, and why?

How can you be more child-like in your faith and in forgiveness?

Pray and ask The Lord to help you become more like this today.

www.ingramcontent.com/pod-product-compliance
Lightning Source LLC
LaVergne TN
LVHW051059080426
835508LV00019B/1974